180 Degrees

Robert

2009

ISBN: 978-1-934379-47-9

"I swear to tell the truth, the whole truth, and nothing but the truth, so help me God."

Buy this book on-line at:
www.the180book.com

For every book purchased, one is donated.

Acknowledgments

I would like to thank all the men and women in the rooms of Alcoholics Anonymous.

I would like to also thank my mentors: Mike Ferry, Anthony Robbins, Dr. Wayne Dyer, The Dalai Lama, Neale Donald Walsch, Brian Tracy, Stephen Covey, Eckhart Tolle, Robert Kiyosaki, Richard Carlson, Napoleon Hill, Norman Vincent Peale, Deepak Chopra, Martin Schwartz, Dr. Phil McGraw, Rhonda Byrne, Lama Surya Das, Marianne Williamson and Og Mandino for helping me become the man I am today.

I also want to thank my friends and family for their support in the writing of this book: my wife, Halle and my son, Skyler, Dieter T., Ginger Coffey, Debra Erdman, Al, Anita, Robert H. and especially Lisa Grantham for the work she did with the first rewrite. Each did their own special part to make this book possible.

This book is dedicated to anyone suffering from drug or alcohol addiction. It is for those wishing for a life free from bondage—a life filled with peace and prosperity.

Forward

Over the years, friends, family, and acquaintances alike have encouraged me to inspire others by sharing the story of my life. I am honoring their support with this book and hoping that it will reach those who need to hear its message the most. No matter how far down the drug or alcohol rat hole you have gone, there is hope and a way out and to find success in all areas of your life spiritually, physically, emotionally, mentally, and financially.

I lived this story, and I am revealing the ugly truth of my own addiction and the story of my recovery to encourage anyone in the terrible grip of addiction to seek help. I hope my story will also inspire those already in recovery to continue their journey.

The title, *180 Degrees*, describes my path to recovery. I turned my life around 180 degrees. I went from being a daily-using drug addict and occasional "big shot" dealer to, eventually, a homeless addict living on the streets. Today I am a completely sober, self-reliant, self-employed husband, father, and self-made millionaire. I was able to miraculously transform my life before I turned thirty.

I escaped the nightmare and created a life beyond my wildest dreams. It wasn't easy, but I am, however, living proof that it can be done. Since drug and alcohol addiction breed tragedy, I am certain there are others whose stories are much worse than mine. I also firmly believe that this message of change and possibility applies to everyone experiencing the nightmare of addiction.

After years of studying my mentors, I have adopted many of

their methods for self-transformation and created some of my own. In this book, I strive to communicate what they have taught me and what I have learned through my own experience. I hope this will help you achieve your own metamorphosis.

Part I of this book is the story of my miserable life as a daily drug user. In Part II, I share my story of getting sober and present the lessons I have learned from my own life experience and the lessons I learned from others.

Getting sober was the first step I took toward achieving all of my dreams and goals.

Anyone currently abusing alcohol and/or drugs has limited chances for success in life. An active addict *may* acquire *some* wealth or earn *limited* achievements but, most likely, will not find a life of peace. Drug and alcohol abuse strips the addict of that opportunity.

Once I achieved sobriety, I was able to create the life I'd always wanted. Today, I have a calm and healthy life filled with love, security, friends, health, fun, peace, and, yes, wealth! I want the same for you, and it is all possible! A wonderful life is out there waiting for you! It is not easy, but it is much easier than the alternative. Working hard to better my life is so much easier than working hard to overcome the problems I created for myself while active in my addiction. I used to live with so much shame and guilt about the actions I'd taken and the loved ones I'd hurt. Living in sobriety is far more rewarding and pleasurable than chasing a drug-induced high. Chasing that high led me down some pitiful paths, and at the end of those paths, I was barely recognizable, but I came back from that life and so can you. Anyone can create the life they desire! I hope that this book inspires you to go after your dreams and make them happen.

180 Degrees

Part I

CHAPTER 1
AGE 20

I remember the night my girlfriend, Tammy, finally left me—or rather, I remember the anguish I felt the morning after. Later that night, I hit another bottom. I'd spent the entire, seemingly eternal, night freebasing alone in my apartment. I'd smoked so much rock that I was completely freaked out and paranoid. I literally walked around the apartment in circles, spun out of my mind, repeatedly checking every window for signs that the cops were staking the place. I had thoroughly convinced myself that Tammy had called the police and "narced" on me. I was sure that *they* were just outside the building, probably scaling up the side of it, preparing to surge in the windows and bust me. I was insane!

The darkness outside eventually slipped into light. I had hardly noticed the dawn breaking, but the sun had come up and the cops had not come. As it got brighter outside, it got darker inside of me. I was so depressed. I was finally out of drugs and forced to come down, which is never a pleasant experience. To make matters worse, I was still too whacked out to do anything about it. There is nothing worse than desperately needing more drugs and being too far gone to know how to get them. I could not leave my apartment, and I was too paranoid to use the phone because I was sure the police had tapped it.

As a typical last resort, I began combing the floor for pieces of blow that may have haphazardly fallen while I was partying. It happens. And none of us who've been there are too proud to get on our hands and knees to weed through the fibers of the carpet for salvation when the situation calls for it. I was a starving rat, searching feverishly for any morsel I could find.

I finally found a grayish-yellow speck that looked like a rock of cocaine. It had just a tinge of white and was the right texture. My spirits soared! It didn't come off the floor when I pulled it, however, and, for just a second, it occurred to me that I might be peeling off a piece of the linoleum. I quickly dismissed the thought because it was too disappointing. It had to be blow! I threw it in my pipe and lit it. It snapped, crackled, tasted horrible, and burned my lungs. It didn't get me high! It must have been the linoleum. I was crushed!

This was another ultimate low. I'd certainly gone to some extremes to get high in the past. I'd slammed cocaine with rum, drunk glasses of rubbing alcohol mixed with Kool-Aid, smoked freebase out of plastic bongs that burned my lungs with each inhale until they melted in my hands, and I'd chugged bottles of Nyquil. Those were all low points for me as an addict, but at least those times, my efforts had eventually succeeded. I'd gotten high all those other times. This time was worse because I'd humiliated myself and still failed.

All I could do was cry. I curled up in a fetal position on the floor of that kitchen and cried like a baby. I was too high to leave and too high to call anyone, but not high enough to feel good. **All I wanted was to stop feeling that way.** It was one of the most miserable, deplorable moments of my life. Yet, sadly, I was still not ready to quit.

CHAPTER 2
AGE 6 – 8

My family lived in Orange County, California, the WASP capital of the world. I was the older of two boys and a part of what seemed to be the perfect family. My mother was an attractive blonde and my father, an attorney, was a strapping and handsome ex-USC football player. From the outside, my family looked like "The American Dream." The inside was a different story all together.

There was a lack of love in my family, and I grew up fearing my father. Consequently, as a child, I felt a deep sadness. My sadness was so deep that by the age of six I was writing suicide letters to my parents. I would cut myself and drip blood all over the pages for added drama. The letters were not empty threats. I made several child-like attempts to kill myself before I was seven. My parents sent me to see many different psychologists, each of whom, I'm told, determined that I was too "too serious" a child.

My brother, Brett, and I were absolutely terrified of our father. We had reason to be. My dad brutally beat us by hand, brush, or belt most nights when he got home—with or without "good reason." Our mother often provoked our father's rage by giving reports of our "bad" behavior. The most troubling memories I have surrounding the abuse deal with the times when we hid in a closet or under our beds, tearfully pleading with our mother to not tell our father of our misbehavior. Although she knew the consequences of her reports, she never granted us mercy. The lashings we received were so severe we often had difficulty walking afterwards. The oppression and trauma in our home continued until the law intervened. Child Protective Services finally came to our aid.

I clearly remember the events that led up to the intervention of Child Protective Services and to my father's subsequent departure. Brett, my brother, had locked me out of the house. He was teasing me from behind a sliding glass door, laughing and joking that he was not going to let me in. I was yelling back at him when my father raced up behind Brett and threw him violently aside. He flung the door open and grabbed me by the throat. The fury I saw in his eyes and the force with which he choked me was horrifying. I can still feel the terror that gripped me in that instant. My father heaved me headfirst through the air and my face collided with the leg of the chair my grandmother was sitting in. I lost consciousness upon impact.

"You bastard!" My grandmother's hysterical scream woke me. I felt the sting from a gash on my forehead as I lifted my head to see what was happening. My grandmother was on the phone. She'd called the authorities and was reporting my father's abuse. His reign of terror was over. My father packed up quickly and walked out of our lives. I wouldn't see him again for seven years.

* * *

My father was not the only predator I had the misfortune of knowing during my childhood. During Dad's last year with us, a babysitter, a seventeen-year-old boy who lived next door, also made his mark on my childhood.

My brother and I looked up to him, and naturally, we were eager to gain his approval. We had a fort in our backyard. He suggested we all "hang out" in the fort together. We thought nothing of it until he literally let it all "hang out"—exposing his penis to us. He masturbated in front of us until he ejaculated. We never told anyone about it because he told us it was a secret that he could make his penis do that. One night when he was babysitting us, he made us get naked and jump up and down on the bed while he watched us. Although both incidents made me very uncomfortable, I didn't say anything to my parents. I sought his approval, and I did not want to be considered a tattle-tale. Brett, however, told our parents, and Dad stormed over to the neighbors' house to talk with the boy's parents. He threatened to kill their son if he so much as looked in our direction again. We never saw the kid again.

I was deeply distressed about these incidents for years. I felt responsible for allowing this abuse to happen. I was upset with myself for not stopping the boy. Also, I regretted that it was my younger brother who had informed my parents of the incidents. It should have been me.

While these traumatic events may have contributed to my destructive and addictive behavior later on, I know of many others with drug problems who came from "normal" families. Their relationships with their parents and loved ones were healthy. Family and upbringing does not necessarily determine the path to addiction.

CHAPTER 3
AGE 9 - 14

Brett, Mom, and I remained together after Dad left. She was only twenty-nine years old, and Brett and I were just seven and nine. Mom hadn't been employed in years and, considering the circumstances, did the best she could to provide for us. She found a job with a travel agency in Los Angeles, and so we left Orange County and moved to an apartment in Brentwood, California.

Our apartment was across the street from Barrington Park, and the years we spent there were some of the happiest of my life. We lived in a two-bedroom apartment that was smaller than any of the homes we'd lived in with Dad, but we didn't have to worry about his temper anymore, so we didn't care. We gladly exchanged luxury for peace. My brother and I asked Mom each night if Dad was coming home, and we were comforted each night when she assured us that he was not.

We struggled financially during those years. Brett and I often made friends with kids from the park who wanted to come home with us for lunch. Mom quickly put a stop to those invitations. She told us that we couldn't afford to feed the whole neighborhood. We could scarcely afford to feed ourselves, and we survived for a couple of years on nothing but soup and sandwiches for dinner.

Toward the end of our second year there, Brett and I were swimming in the apartment complex pool one afternoon when we met Josh. He and his mom, Judy, had just moved into the complex. We all became close friends immediately. Judy was also a single mom trying to make ends meet, and we soon found ourselves living amicably as two families in a two-bedroom apartment. Sharing expenses made sense because we all got along so well.

Barrington Park was our home away from home for several years. Josh, Brett, and I spent our time playing sports and games there after school and on weekends. We knew all the other neighborhood kids and all the park employees. We thought the older kids who hung around the park were cool. We watched these older kids with great interest, and eventually, we began to notice things that led us to believe that some of the rumors we'd heard about the older kids were true. Some of the boys we respected and admired were using drugs. I was torn between being impressed and being wary. I had promised my mom and my grandmother that I would never do drugs because of the trouble my aunt and uncle had gotten into with their drug use (The effect of my aunt and uncle's drug use figures prominently later in my story). I managed to keep that promise for a few more years.

When I was about twelve years old, my mom met Sam. Sam lived on a horse ranch in the San Fernando Valley, and she eventually decided to marry him. My brother and I were shocked when we found out that we had to leave our friends and our familiar stomping grounds to live on an isolated horse ranch in Chatsworth. The only thing that made the situation bearable was that Judy and Josh moved there with us. They were unable to afford their own rent without my mom's contribution.

Initially, Josh, Brett, and I attended a small, newly-formed private school down the street from the ranch in Chatsworth. I'm not sure how Mom and Sam were able to afford it, but they did for a couple of years. Just like my elementary school years in Orange County and Brentwood, I was an exemplary student, and after school, I was involved in extracurricular activities like bike riding and sports. Josh, Brett, and I played with the other kids from the time school let out until dusk. Then we'd go home, have dinner, and finish our homework. We were ideal children.

After elementary school, that situation began to change. I was introduced to punk rock the summer before I started junior high. I jumped into it enthusiastically. I think that all the opposition surrounding punk rock made it attractive to me. Plus, punk rockers stood out in a crowd. They got noticed. During my early punk days, my relationship with my mom began to veer off track. She started implying that I was on drugs. At the time, I was not. She forbade me from going out on several occasions because she believed that anyone who dressed like I did and who listened to that music had to be doing drugs. We began fighting after a few of these episodes.

I began thinking, "If I am being accused of doing drugs and getting punished for doing them, well then, I might as well do them!" At the time, I did not act on that thought, though her insinuations were infuriating.

Junior high marked the beginning of a whole new world for me. I was at a new school, had a new image and reputation, made new friends, and discovered girls. Reflecting back on my initial drug use, I realize now that the main reason I began using drugs was to feel accepted, especially by the girls I liked. But I confess, I was also tired of being treated like a drug user before I had even tried drugs.

All of the girls I was interested in partied, and I did not want to be the dork that did not. Partying with the girls gave me the opportunity to spend time with them. We would hang out at "The Stump," an old tree stump in the middle of an empty lot adjacent to the schoolyard. This is when, in my mind, I went from being the "goody-two-shoes dork" to the "cool partier."

I was still in control in the beginning. During my first and only year at that junior high school, I only partied a little. I smoked pot and drank every once in a while. One time I even tried mushrooms, but I did not have enough, apparently, to get high. For the most part, I was just a recreational partier. **Later, when my addictions had spun out of control, I tried fruitlessly to recreate this period of relatively "innocent" drug use.**

The summer after that pivotal school year, I heard from Dad for the first time since his hasty departure seven years earlier. He called to let us know he was living in the San Francisco Bay Area and that he would like Brett and me to come visit him. Hoping he had changed, we did. He was living in Cupertino, a city in the South Bay, closer to San Jose than San Francisco. He had a nice house in a decent area, much better than the ranch, and while we were there, he did everything he could to impress us. He was extravagant with his money and lenient with us—two very likable qualities in a father. He bought us gifts and allowed us to stay out late. He was trying to make up for being such a lousy father.

Dad had experienced a lot of financial success early in his career. He and Mom had enjoyed a lavish lifestyle when Brett and I were very young. For whatever reason, though, Dad lost it all just prior to the violent episode that led to his departure. I do not know if this financial shift is what led to the increase in domestic violence. In the seven years since we had seen him, he had somehow regained his stature, and he wanted us to notice. He had reclaimed some of his wealth, had a new wife, Misty, and wanted his sons back in his life.

That summer in Cupertino, Brett and I enjoyed many liberties. The loose purse strings and lax rules created a virtual utopia for two teenage boys. When the time came to go back down south, I decided to call Cupertino my new home. There was no way I was leaving that situation. I was staying with Dad. Part of me wanted the opportunity to finally have a father-son relationship, but another part really just did not like Chatsworth. Of course, the major reason I wanted to stay was self-serving. I saw that if

I stayed behind, I could have anything I wanted. Dad was in a perfect position to be manipulated. Brett left for LA, and I stayed to start a whole new life with Dad.

CHAPTER 4
AGE 14 - 15

I began taking my first steps down the dark road of addiction. Dad continued to spoil me by giving me whatever I wanted and by letting me go out and do whatever I wanted. It was a disastrous combination, particularly at this stage in my life. The partier mentality I was developing thrived in my new environment. Along with a new home and school, I acquired a reputation. I was known as a crazy stoner/ punk rocker from LA, which suited me well. I had a white Mohawk haircut and sported an earring.

I enjoyed the notoriety that came with my image and found myself trying to live up to people's expectations. This, of course, was extremely fun because it meant that I had no boundaries. My drug use escalated. **My genetic predisposition to addiction and my addictive personality took control of my life.** I progressed from an occasional partier to a daily drug user, as easily as I moved from Southern California to Northern. I spent the first half of my freshman year either smoking pot or drinking beer every day, depending on what was available. If both were available, I was happy. Although I wasn't old enough to buy alcohol and I didn't have a lot of extra cash, it wasn't that difficult to keep a surplus of "party supplies" on hand. We all had access to our parents' liquor cabinets. Marijuana was even easier to come by than booze. When funds and supplies ran low, we pooled our resources.

By the time I'd completed my first semester at Cupertino High, I was a seasoned partier and, therefore, in my mind, ready to try the harder drugs I was being offered. I'd decided that drugs were drugs. Why not use whatever I could get my hands on? The floodgates opened. I dropped acid (LSD) fairly early in my drug-using career. My friend Bill warned me before I took it that I would never be the same again. He said that one hit would alter my personality forever, and that I could even go crazy. He knew of someone who'd gone nuts after a trip and never recovered. I took the hit anyway. Looking back, it blows my mind that, despite being advised of the risks and possible consequences, I still chose to take it. Believing I could lose my mind, my personality, *myself*, I did it anyway.

I still remember that first acid trip, at least some of it. It was late afternoon and I was with three friends. We dosed at a bowling alley called *Futurama*. Soon after we started tripping, we left the bowling alley and ducked into some bushes along the expressway to smoke a bowl of buds. The traffic along the Lawrence Expressway moves fast and is not meant for pedestrians. Nevertheless, it surprised us when a policeman was suddenly on top of us, shining a flashlight in our faces. "Hold it! Police!" he yelled. Tripping and totally stoned, we reacted the way any delinquent kids would. We ran! My friends bolted down one path and got away. I took off and found myself dodging speeding traffic as I tried to cut across the expressway. It was twilight and headlights glared all around me. Vivid rays of light shot at me like lasers, leaving trails in their wake. All my senses were heightened and, in addition to the brilliant streaks of light, I could hear the hum of car engines and the swish of wind whipping by with each passing vehicle.

Reality doesn't sink in very quickly when you are tripping on acid. Everything is liquid and flowing. The trees and bushes move with the ground, rising and falling, as if they're breathing. It is a surrealistic experience. It feels as if you can rewind and replay a scenario if the outcome is unfavorable. I felt like the director of a movie, at liberty to yell, "Cut!" or "Take two! Let's try that again without the car hitting me!" I was lucky. I didn't have to find out the hard way that, despite my feelings of omnipotence, my reality could not be manipulated so easily.

The next thing I knew I was in the middle of the highway. Suddenly, I was aware that this was not a video game. I dashed for the shoulder of the road. Bright lights were headed right for me. Totally blinded by them, I leapt out of the way of what sounded like a semi. A rush of air clipped my backside. The speeding truck missed me by a dangerously narrow margin as I jumped off the overpass and tumbled ten to fifteen feet down a steep hill. At the end of the drop, I rolled another twenty feet along the landscaped hillside of the off ramp before coming to a stop in the middle of the road. I scurried to my feet and out of traffic as cars honked and people yelled, staring at me in disbelief. It took me a couple of minutes to shake off the fall and dust off my clothes. Then I began to laugh hysterically. I could have been arrested, injured, or killed, but I found the whole scenario deliriously funny.

I rejoined my cohorts back at the bowling alley. They shared the details of their escapades with me, and I recounted my adventure to them. They found it, as well as the grass and dirt stains all over me, as amusing as I did. Once the laughter subsided, I suggested we all go out and smoke a bowl. We all looked at each other, trying to determine which of us had the bag of weed. Then, we realized that none of us had grabbed the pot when the cop interrupted us. Now that wasn't funny! I was so mad and disappointed, but my anger and disappointment made no sense. When tripping on acid, smoking pot and drinking have very little effect. The effects of acid are dominant. It is futile to take any other drug to get higher during a trip.

"I'm going back to get the bag," I announced with conviction. The hilarity started up again at the absurdity of my proposal.

Not only would I have to cross the expressway again, but I'd have to find the exact spot in the bushes where we'd been. I'd have to do it all in the dark and avoid the cop. It was an insane undertaking with very little promise of success. Yet, I was able to accomplish the mission.

We celebrated in ceremonial style and smoked the whole eighth of bud that evening. Later we managed to break into a mobile home on a sales lot and settle in for the night. We smoked, laughed, and tripped all night long. Suddenly, it was morning, and we heard voices outside the camper. One of the people talking sounded like a salesman. We could hear him describing the camper to a potential buyer. Much to their surprise, a cloud of smoke and a group of stoned teenagers greeted them when they opened the door. We calmly gathered our things, politely excused ourselves, and exited the camper. Then, we headed up the road, three of us on my little moped and one of us on a skateboard. That first of hundreds of acid trips launched my commitment to a life of drinking, drugs, and drama.

CHAPTER 5
AGE 15

I was having a blast in my new life. I liked my new home, my new parents, my popularity, and my scene at school. I loved being known as a partier and was thoroughly enjoying my "punk rocker from LA" reputation. I thrived on the attention. I also liked the duplicity of my image. No one thought of me as the drug addict (at first), because I was also an athlete. I was a football player. I appeared to be a wholesome high school jock who liked to party. But my football jersey was a disguise. My parents, teachers, and peers didn't see past my athletic façade. The long-haired guys who wore the heavy metal concert t-shirts and smoked pot occasionally had worse reputations, but I was the one doing drugs every day.

For the most part, I avoided high school. I was constantly ditching class, or I was completely stoned if I was there. I spent my first few days at Cupertino High sitting in classes I didn't belong in because I was too wasted to raise my hand and ask to be escorted to the correct class. Then, when the class was dismissed, I roamed the hallways, lost, until I randomly selected another classroom to enter, again not knowing which class I was attending.

As my freshman year at Cupertino progressed, my reputation as the jock/punk/partier began to fade. I was being labeled the punk/drug addict instead. I could have kept the jock/partier image going longer if I'd chosen to spend more time with the jocks, but their occasional beer drinking gigs were way too boring and amateurish for me. I started breaking away from the team and hanging out with guys who did harder drugs. The transition was relatively easy because I was really already one of them. My punk rock Mohawk and earring helped me make fast friends with the hard-core rockers, metal heads, burnouts, and cruisers, because we all stood out in some way, as opposed to the more mainstream preps, cheerleaders, jocks, and geeks. Most importantly, of course, my new friends and I shared a common bond—drugs.

Within this group of new friends there were the casual partiers and the true partiers—the drug addicts. **For a true addict, there comes a time when the desire to do drugs or drink alcohol progresses from "if it's around" to "liking it" to "wanting it" to "needing it."** At this point in my drug career, I was in the "wanting it" stage.

I hung out regularly with other daily users, and we did everything and anything to keep the flow of drugs going. We kept mental records of who was holding drugs and how much. The core group of us would share with each other because we knew we were in this thing together—we were committed to *getting high daily*. It was obvious to us that a collaborative effort to stay high would more likely guarantee success than "going it alone."

Doing drugs with people who partied as much as I did helped me stay in denial about "being an addict." Back then, none of us would have ever used the term "addict." That was too revealing, too honest. We called ourselves "partiers" and were proud that something set us apart from the lame jock and cheerleader crowd.

It was only a few months into my first year at Cupertino that I started using cocaine and crank (meth). Until then, I had experimented with acid and mushrooms and routinely smoked pot and drank. But booze and weed became too ordinary and boring, and tripping on acid too many times a week made it difficult to function. Good ol' blow (cocaine) came to the rescue. At first, blow was something to look forward to, something to use only occasionally because it was expensive. However, as any good drug addict discovers, there is never enough of a good thing.

I quickly figured out that the only way to maintain a sufficient supply of coke and pot to keep me happy was to deal it to others. I deduced that I would be able to sell to my friends and anyone else and keep some for myself for free. I supplied myself with drugs for the entirety of my using career by dealing, scamming, and stealing. When I began selling, I crossed over into the stage of "needing to get high." My addiction was off and running.

I grew increasingly angry as my freshman year drew to a close. I assume it was a combination of early childhood memories, all the drugs I was doing, and my submersion into the punk rock scene. Being a punk rocker didn't necessarily mean you *had* to be angry, but there was a pervasive rebelliousness in the music, lyrics, and style that encouraged an indignant attitude. I grew increasingly hateful toward the world and society. The suicidal thoughts I'd had as a child returned. I was constantly wondering about the point of life. As I became more incensed and malevolent, I paid closer attention to the words in the punk and heavy metal music. I began to feel and live the angry music.

The more horrific the lyrics, the more hateful I became. The songs were all about anarchy, murder, death, and the Devil. I started accepting and, to a degree, worshipping the Devil. I was drawn to anything akin to demons, hate, anarchy, and death. My life was consumed with evil thoughts. I wore clothes adorned with demonic symbols or scenes of death and murder. I wrote songs for my friends' band about devil worship and murder. I used metal nails to dig upside down crosses, "FTW" (Fuck The World), and anarchy symbols into my flesh. I'd let the blood drip down my arms and stain my clothes. The scabs became emblems declaring my enmity. I wore upside down crosses as earrings and charms. I felt hollow and dark inside. My veins ran with venom. I was lost—completely lost.

A friend, Scott, told me that his sister and her boyfriend were Satan worshippers. He said his sister was a witch and her boyfriend was a warlock. This totally intrigued me. In fact, I was envious and wanted to know all about them. Scott told stories about the black magic they were capable of, the black masses they attended in the mountains, and the virgin women they sacrificed. Participants committed gruesome acts to please the Devil such as raping the virgins' blood-covered bodies and drinking their blood and eating their flesh. The purpose of these acts was to increase their "black magic power" by gaining favor with the Devil.

These stories shocked and horrified me but fascinated me as well. A part of me wanted to attend a black mass and witness the depravity firsthand. It was the same kind of twisted compulsion I felt to watch horror movies or turn my head to see the results of a car accident. Another part of me feared that I might be dark enough to participate. I never took that chance.

Looking back, it saddens and disgusts me that I was so compelled by this dark culture. I am so thankful that I never did attend a black mass or participate in anything resembling one. I am ashamed that I was someone who was intrigued by the most horrific acts imaginable.

CHAPTER 6
AGE 15

Any interest I'd had in the demonic realm ended one night when I was on acid. I was down south visiting my mom and brother in LA. Tripping with Brett and some friends up in the hills around Chatsworth, we came across a closed and boarded up church at a cemetery and broke into it. We found some wine inside that, considering the dilapidated state of the church, must have been quite old. Some of the guys drank it anyway, and later that night, they were very sick.

After we left the church, we went back up in the hills and began rock climbing in the dark. We heard a helicopter approaching. The sound grew louder and louder, and we saw a spotlight sweeping across the nearby hillside. We realized that the police were looking for us. The caretaker from the cemetery had heard us in the church and called the police. The searchlight swept back and forth across the rough terrain as we hurdled from rock to rock, trying to stay out of sight.

Earlier that year, I had injured my knee playing football, and so during this acid trip, I was wearing a brace and using crutches. I didn't have any business hiking in the dark in the first place, never mind running and vaulting from rock to rock along a hillside. I remember hearing my knee crack every once in a while, and it seemed to dislodge with each crack. I knew I was hurting it, but for the most part, I ignored it.

From rock to rock, we blindly leapt without any idea where we were going to land. At one point, a friend named Keith and I took cover together. Keith was one of the guys who'd drunk some of the old wine, and he was sick. He was a tall, lanky guy, thin as a rail, with long, straight, naturally white hair. Keith was ordinarily very pale, but that night, because he was ill, his skin was grayish blue.

Keith and I were hiding between two boulders when the helicopter flew overhead and shone its searchlight just above us. As light shot through the crevices between the rocks, I looked up at Keith. His ghostly face was illuminated. His grayish-blue skin looked translucent, and his long white hair flared out all around him, whipping in the wind. He was just staring at me with this sick look on his face. I was tripping on his long white hair. His eerie appearance and the madness of what was happening intensified the hit of acid I'd taken. I started to trip—big time!

I became convinced that I was being possessed by the Devil, and that Keith was one of the Devil's children. The heavy metal band Iron Maiden has a mascot named Eddie. I used to draw pictures of Eddie killing people all the time. That night, Keith became Eddie, and I was sure he had come to get me. I was certain that God was finished with me. I'd already angered Him by flirting with the Devil, and now He'd had it. This was it. He'd tolerated my fascination with Satan, but breaking into the church had been the last straw. I had desecrated His house. I began to really freak out.

I had taken acid a number of times before and was experienced enough to know how to placate myself, if needed. I knew how distorted reality could get, so I kept telling myself to chill. I reassured myself that Keith was not Eddie, and that he was not going to kill me. I kept telling myself that I was not cursed. Despite all my efforts to remain calm and rational, I was terrified.

I'm not sure how much time went by, but it seemed like an

eternity. We were all able to get away from the cops, and I was finally able to get away from Keith. Back at Mom's house later that night, Brett and I went to his room to listen to tunes and crash. I turned my attention to my injured knee. I was certain I'd done some damage to it, and I wanted to investigate the extent of the damage. I undid the leg brace and discovered that my knee was totally swollen. Tentatively, I touched the kneecap and found that it appeared to be floating loosely above the slush of fluid and cartilage. It nauseated me. When I stood up to walk to the bathroom, the entire room began to spin. I stumbled my way to the bathroom and fell to the floor. The room was whirling like a satellite out in space, spinning in every direction. It was totally uncontrollable. I closed my eyes to keep the room from revolving, but then I saw hallucinations of Eddie screaming at me, threatening to take over my mind, body, and soul. I felt I was going insane! Eddie was alternately laughing and screaming at me. His face kept changing, first melting away as if it were made of wax, and then reforming as if being molded from clay. I was convinced that the Devil had taken control of me. It was the scariest drug experience I ever had.

I spent the rest of that night curled up in a fetal position on the floor of the bathroom crying. Each time I closed my eyes, I saw the demonic face of Eddie, and every time I opened my eyes to stop this hallucination, the room would whirl about uncontrollably, again making me nauseous. When I woke up the next morning, it had all stopped. And once it was over, I knew that I had not been possessed by the Devil. This event, however, transformed me.

When I got back home to my dad's house, I threw away everything I had that represented the Devil or that resembled anything satanic. I asked Dad to buy me a cross to wear around my neck, and I started going to church with him—not always, but often. I begged God for forgiveness and promised Him I would never turn my back on Him again. Having done this, I felt somewhat saved.

CHAPTER 7
AGE 15 - 16

In my second year of high school, I was selling and doing drugs daily. I could easily get any drug anyone wanted. On a typical school day, I had a couple ounces of buds and a couple grams of blow on me, weighed out and ready to sell. I kept special orders, ounces of mushrooms and hits of acid, at home in my closet. This year, I took my drug use to another level. I began shooting cocaine.

One evening while I was snorting lines with a couple of guys, Mark and Robbie, one of them asked me if I knew why blow was so expensive. When I told him I didn't, he explained that it was because of the high that slamming (shooting) it produced. For the record, I am afraid of needles. I hate them. Even today, I pass out when I get my blood checked. On that night, however, I was a little drunk and, therefore, a little gutsier than usual. More importantly, I wanted to know what that kind of high was like. So I agreed to do it.

Mark and Robbie told me to stick my arm out, underside up, and to clench and unclench my fist several times so they could easily find a vein. Mark gripped his fists around my arm and blew on the place where the needle was going to go in. I turned my head away so that I could not see what was happening, and I barely felt the needle that Robbie stuck into my arm. I immediately felt the rush of cocaine to my head.

My entire head felt like it was freezing up and my ears popped. The roof of my mouth and the back of my throat filled up with the incredible taste of cocaine. I felt like my head was inside a bell that was ringing gently, and the sound waves were reverberating as if I was underwater. My heart pounded rapidly, but everything else slowed down. I was in heaven. I was high!

That was the first of dozens of pokes that night. My arms were pincushions by the next morning. I could not get enough. The high from snorting cocaine lasts at least a half an hour or so. The rush from shooting is over in less than ten minutes. I just wanted to keep shooting. We slammed blow all night long.

I had to attend a pancake breakfast for the varsity football team the next morning with Dad. It was a joke. There I was, a sophomore, sitting with the varsity players and my dad, trying to eat pancakes after having slammed cocaine all night long. I hadn't slept a wink. My eyes were bloodshot slits with pinpoint pupils. I could hardly tolerate light. My mouth was so dry that I could not swallow the pancakes. I chewed and chewed, tried to swallow without success, and literally gagged at the table. I don't know how I was able to pull it off, but somehow, I managed the event without raising too much suspicion. There were a few whispered queries, "What the hell is wrong with Rob?" but nothing to raise an alarm.

Coming down after shooting cocaine is a nightmare. The crash is crippling. It's like being shoved off a cliff and plummeting into a deep chasm. The depression is uncontrollable and accompanied by irrepressible and irrational anger. You're really pissed that someone shoved you off the cliff! I was torn between crying, screaming, and tearing apart anything and everything in sight. And while the high is fleeting, coming down from it takes some time. Most times, I just tried to wait it out. Struggling with paranoia, I would sit and stare out a window or at a door. I was just trying to survive. It was sheer torture. **Still, this excruciating**

aftermath wasn't sufficient to deter me from doing it again and again. Sadly, at the time, that initial rush continued to be worth any misery I was forced to endure in the "come down" or from the chaos I was creating in my life.

That was the first of many nights of slamming coke and the first of many mornings-after when I had to pay the price. Like any good addict, I was always looking for the easy way around the hard part. Coming down from cocaine was the hard part, so when I was introduced to heroin, I immediately recognized the benefits. Heroin was the easy way down from coke because it is a downer that counters the extreme paranoia created by shooting cocaine. The main reason I tried it was to come down from slamming blow. Initially, we mixed it with whatever blow was left at the end of the night. We would cook up a speedball to end our session.

CHAPTER 8
AGE 16

Slamming cocaine and heroin dominated my life. Every thought, every action was motivated by the need for more. When I was on a run, I would do just about anything to feed my arms. **I was a slave to the drugs.** Nothing was worse than running out of drugs. Once I had more, I'd slam it in an excited frenzy. I was like a starving dog, snarling and impatient.

    I slammed blow by whatever means necessary. I shared needles with guys I suspected had diseases. I used dirty needles, needles used by strangers. I sharpened old dull needles the best I could and had to practically dig them into my arms. I even used a bent needle, one I'd tried to break in a failed attempt to stop. I shot dope with all kinds of people in all kinds of places: cars, alleys, gas station bathrooms, and even classic prep parties at school. I continued slamming cocaine until my girlfriend asked me if I was doing heroin. She'd heard from people at school that I was, and she wanted to know if it was true. **Like any good addict, I looked right into her eyes and lied.** I not only denied it, I became indignant about the insulting accusation.

    That rumor marked the beginning of my troubles at Cupertino High. I was sitting in the back of my Biology class when the school narcotic agents entered the room and approached the teacher. I knew they were there for me. They were going to pull me out of class and take me to Mr. Sena's office for another body and locker search. Without hesitation, I quickly removed all the drugs I had hidden in my socks and underwear and handed them to Mike, the jock sitting next to me. Mike was a sound choice for this hand-off for several reasons. He was seated right next to me, but more importantly, he was safe. My drugs would be safe with him. Mike was an honest, nice guy, and didn't party at all. I knew I would get everything back untouched. I quickly handed him multiple bags of buds and mushrooms and several bindles of blow. My intuition proved correct. Seconds after the hand-off, I was called to the head of the class and escorted out.

The most intense part of this particular incident was that I had dropped a hit of acid at lunch and I was just starting to trip. I had to concentrate on each and every step I took between the classroom and the office and had difficulty not bursting into laughter. I knew that if I even snickered, I'd explode into hysterics. At one point, I considered running for it to postpone the situation until I was more mentally prepared but decided against it. I was having enough trouble just walking.

When I got to the principal's office, the agent frisked me. I wondered if I had removed everything, and evidently I had. Mr. Sena informed me that my stepmother was coming to pick me up. I felt an immediate sense of relief. This wasn't a drug bust after all. This was something else entirely. I casually walked out to the front of the school with a big smile on my face and waited for Misty to pull up, very pleased that I was going to get to enjoy the rest of my trip.

When my stepmother arrived, I hopped into her car, turned on some music, and enthusiastically asked what was up. Misty simply replied that she was taking me to see Dad at his office, and no, she didn't know why. Although I was curious, I couldn't do much more than listen to the music, watch the scenery, and enjoy my trip. When I arrived at Dad's office, he asked me to close the door behind me. The moment I did, he hit me with the question,

"How long have you been doing brown?"

I was so surprised by his question. I'm sure I looked stupid too. I was staring at him, slack-jawed and perplexed, wondering how he knew what "brown" was and kissing my high good-bye. And how did he find out I was doing heroin? How was I going to get out of this one? And most importantly, could someone just hit the pause button on this whole fucking downer scene and allow me to go back to enjoying my dose? "What are you talking about?" I asked, like any good addict would. "I have no idea what 'brown' is!" I said this with absolute sincerity, wondering if the pop marks on my arm were still noticeable.

He said, "Don't play dumb with me. Brown is heroin. Jack told me all about your drug use." Jack was a neighborhood kid. Then he asked, "Who are Mark, Robbie, and Don?"

While I was playing ignorant and denying any knowledge of these people, he threw several pictures out on his desk for me to see. They were photographs of me entering Mark, Robbie and Don's homes on different occasions. He revealed that he had hired a private detective to follow me. Before I could formulate a response, a voice interjected from the speakerphone on my dad's desk. It totally freaked me out because I was still high. It was a police sergeant friend of Dad's and the man who'd taken the photos. He explained the photos. I was speechless. All I could think was: *Fuck! This is a seriously bad acid trip!* It slowly dawned on me that I'd been caught red-handed. The accusation was substantiated with photographs! Once the shock wore off, I turned to angry denial. How dare my dad believe Jack of all people! And how dare Jack talk to my dad about me! The nerve! I was furious, and I let my dad know it.

"I can't believe you could think I would shoot drugs! I would never do that! You know that I pass out just getting blood drawn! And how could you take Jack's word for anything? He's just a jealous asshole who's pissed off because Dieter (a mutual friend) is spending more time with me than with him. He's in love with Dieter, for God's sake, and he's a fucking dick for using you to try and get me out of the picture! I can't believe you fell for it! He's not going to get away with this!"

As the conversation continued, just like during the confrontation with my girlfriend, I was afraid he would ask me to lift my shirtsleeves. To my absolute amazement and relief, he never did. It was a rookie mistake. It would have been "game over" if he had simply said, "Let me see your arms." Yet, he never requested that simple, obvious thing. Incredible! It got even more ludicrous from there. My dad and his police officer buddy pulled another totally rookie maneuver. They'd set up an appointment for me to have my blood drug tested at a doctor's office. And I was supposed to drive myself there to have it done! It was all I could do to not crack a smile as I agreed. It was the most ridiculous thing I'd ever heard.

When I got back to school, I found Mike and retrieved my stash from him. From there, I went to a friend's house, still tripping and needing to come down and gather my thoughts. Of course, I never went to the doctor's office.

Later that night when I got home, Dad yelled at me and I yelled back. I told him the directions he'd given me were wrong and that I hadn't been able to find the damn office. I told him I had wanted to take the drug test as badly as he wanted me to take it, so that I could prove my innocence. I also let him know how hurt and angry I was that he'd taken someone else's word over his own son's. By the end of that night's dispute, I had convinced Dad that a drug test wasn't necessary because I was not shooting dope. Once again, whether due to my debating skills or to his blind and desperate wish to believe me, I was able to avoid the consequences of my drug use.

The ability to effortlessly develop some quick-witted and truly brilliant responses to justify different awkward

situations is a talent that I believe all drug addicts either have naturally or acquire quickly. I was no exception. I believed this talent was necessary to my survival and to my continued drinking and drug use. **I mastered bullshitting and manipulation as an act of self-preservation.** I was also an excellent actor when the situation demanded a convincing performance to protect my drug use. I put on such stellar performances that I even believed some of them myself.

CHAPTER 9
AGE 16

In the spring of my sophomore year at Cupertino, things at home started getting really bad. I was constantly fighting with Misty and Dad. Misty was always raining on my parade, invariably trying to catch me doing something wrong—and she often did. I constantly denied her accusations, which meant it was her word against mine. Dad was always stuck in the middle while Misty and I blamed each other. I said she was lying, and she said I was. Of course, there was only one liar—me.

They caught me one night. I was confronted with evidence. It's very difficult to dispute evidence, but, of course, I did. I was hanging out with my girlfriend at her parents' house when Dad called. "Stay put. I'm coming to get you," he said. I heard the translation: "Freeze! Put your hands where I can see them." I had my moped with me, so I offered to drive home, but he wanted me to wait there for him. It was an odd request and made me uneasy.

As soon as I got into his car, he handed me the shoebox that I kept in my closet. My stomach sank. The box contained my stash, and at the time, I was holding quite a bit. I didn't have to open it to know what he'd seen. There were bags of weed, a half-ounce of mushrooms, a bottle of Valium, and several bindles of blow. The coup de grace, however, was that, at the time, I also had half a dozen needles in the box too. When backed into a corner, it's best to come out fighting. So that's what I did. I attacked my dad. I know it's shocking, but it's true. I actually had the audacity to turn this around on him.

"I can't believe you went through my stuff!" I yelled. He wasn't taking any flack from me this time, though, and he shut me up quickly. He started throwing my drugs out the window onto the freeway. I thought fast and was able to salvage most of the drugs by telling him they weren't all mine, and that I'd be in serious trouble, physical trouble, if I couldn't produce them later. This was an outright lie, but it sounded good. He considered what I said, and as angry as he was, he didn't want to see me get hurt. He quit throwing the drugs out the window.

I wasn't off the hook yet, though. Next, he accused me of dealing. This was a logical assumption considering the drugs were weighed out and divided into separate bags and bindles. I was at the top of my game, however, and I felt encouraged that I'd been able to save most of the stash. I denied dealing. I told him that the drugs were in different bags because they belonged to different people. I explained that I kept my stash separate so that when I took some to a party I could ration it out. I was amazed at the load of crap I dumped on him. But he believed me, again. This was especially mind-blowing since he had been a narcotics agent in the military. We drove home, and he actually gave me back the rest of the drugs, since he thought they belonged to other people. He kept the needles, saying my friends could replace those themselves. That was certainly fair enough.

Without any consequences, early the next morning I got a ride from Misty back over to my girlfriend's to pick up my moped, which I drove to school. As soon as I got to school, I found some friends and shared the night's events with them. One of them, Steve, had a car so I made him a proposition. If he'd take his car and follow me on my moped in order to slow car traffic along the freeway, I'd be able to find the bags of blow my dad had thrown out the window. I would get him high if I was able to successfully find the bags. Steve went for it.

He drove illegally behind me as I cruised along the expressway, as fast as my moped would take me, looking for my blow. I realize that it sounds like a crazy scheme, but it paid off. I found the bags of blow! I still can't believe I found them or that I was willing to do something so dangerous to get my drugs. As promised, Steve and I got whacked out on the blow we retrieved before going to class that day.

A few months later, I was involved in another incident that made matters even worse for me at home. I had borrowed Dad's car, and three friends and I were sitting in the car in a parking lot at De Anza College. We were doing some blow and had been parked there for some time when there was a knock on the driver's side window. We couldn't see who it was because the windows were all fogged up. I rolled down the window. It was Dieter's dad, and Dieter was in the car with me. His dad wanted to see him and asked that he get out of the car. It was really weird. It shocked us all, Dieter especially, and he reluctantly left with his father. Dieter's dad called me "the Devil." He wasn't the only one who'd used those words when referring to me. I wasn't concerned though; I had my own dad to worry about.

Shortly after the incident with Dieter's father, I was getting high in my dad's car with some friends in that same parking lot. I was leaning back on the car door when it opened abruptly. I fell out of the car and onto a cop. Looking up from the ground, all I could see was the cop's badge and gun. Instinctively, I reached for the blow in my jacket pocket so that I could throw it down, but the cop stopped me. He pulled me to my feet while his partner pulled my friends out of the vehicle.

As I was being cuffed, I noticed Dieter and his dad pulling out of the parking lot, and I knew Dieter was probably able to see what was happening. De Anza's Laser Light Show had just ended, and people were exiting the theater and heading back to their cars. I saw dozens of people I knew from school, and they saw me too. My bust was all over school in no time.

My night in Juvenile Hall sucked! That is an understatement. For the first time I was in a situation where I was not in control of my drug use—and I didn't like it at all! **That night was a major wake-up call for me. Unfortunately, I just hit the snooze button, rolled over, and went back to sleep.** I was *still* not ready to quit. I'm not alone in this experience. There are many addicts who ignore their wake-up calls. Fortunately, we are often given another chance.

The next morning, Dad had me released, but my days at Cupertino were numbered. He was becoming incredibly frustrated. He tried to get me to live in a halfway house, but I wasn't willing to do that. In fact, in the intake interview, when I realized they were trying to get me to stay in a halfway house, I went into a rage, breaking tables and windows and throwing things. I even threw a chair at one of the counselors. After witnessing this behavior, they wouldn't let me stay there anyway.

Dad was at his wit's end, and I was getting close to mine. It was becoming increasingly difficult to keep a surplus of drugs available for my own use. School was out for the summer, so I didn't have the same demand from my regular buyers that I did during the school year. Without buyers, I couldn't supply my own stash. My disposition took a quick turn for the worse.

For my grand finale in the Bay Area, I used Dad's credit card to buy thousands of dollars worth of retail merchandise for a major cocaine dealer in exchange for the equivalent in blow. I did this largely out of anger toward my father, but also to score. Then I told Dad that I wanted to move back to Los Angeles to live with my Mom and Brett. In one day, I suddenly picked up and left all my friends and my girlfriend. I left Cupertino, and all the mess I had created, behind me. I was settled back down south in LA before the credit card bill arrived. It was the last time I saw Dad for a number of years.

CHAPTER 10
AGE 16

I returned to LA an entirely different kid. I was no longer into the punk rock scene, for one thing. I hadn't lost interest in it as much as I'd exhausted it. It didn't offer me anything anymore. That subculture was all about righteous indignation and nonconformity, and I figured that if I was such a hard-core punk, the only avenue available to me was suicide. After all, if life was so miserable and the world so messed up, then why not end it all? But I didn't want my life to end. I was having too much fun getting stoned. In a weird way, drugs might have saved my life because they rescued me from the gloom and doom of the punk scene.

I'd matured in other ways, too, of course. My drug use had advanced and picked up in frequency and intensity. Furthermore, my drug use was starting to create physiological problems. It was impossible for me to eat without smoking pot first. My stomach wouldn't tolerate it. Cuts and sores had developed on the roof of my mouth that made eating and drinking excruciating. I once tried to drink orange juice while the entire top half of my mouth was riddled with cankerous cuts. The pain was so intense that I screamed in agony. It felt like rubbing alcohol was being poured over an open wound in my mouth. I'll never forget it.

The most obvious change, however, was in my physical appearance. I only weighed 110 pounds (down from 150 pounds), and I had sunken gray eyes and bad skin. I was the walking dead. I was taking the prescription drug Accutane for my acne, but my own drug use combined with the medication to make my breakouts even worse. I knew I could have better skin if I'd lay off the drugs, but I couldn't. I looked terrible.

Before I came home, Dad updated Mom about everything she'd missed over the past couple of years. He told her about the drugs he'd found in my closet, my arrest, and my lies. When the credit card bill arrived, he called and told her about that too. While living with Mom, I went to Chatsworth High. I fell in easily with similar kids, and my drug habit never missed a beat. I was still sixteen, but my seventeenth birthday was approaching. I was partying constantly and spent a whole week eating mushrooms and taking acid. I couldn't continue at that pace for much longer. Something had to give.

My mom was worried that I might be planning something excessive for my seventeenth birthday. She feared I would overdose while celebrating it. She begged me to see the same therapist Josh had seen for his drug problems. I checked with Josh, who'd seen the guy to appease his mom, and he said the guy was really cool. Therefore, I agreed to go see him for my mom's sake, although I had an ulterior motive. I did, after all, want to go out and party on my seventeenth birthday, and I'd gotten the impression that she was willing to do anything necessary to prevent me from going out that night. I was afraid she might have me arrested. I was going to have to see this therapist so I told her to go ahead and make the appointment.

The therapist's name was Steve, and he was easily the coolest one I'd ever met. I had been to see dozens of therapists, starting back when I was a suicidal six-year old, but none one of them had made a single relevant point or inspired me in any way. They were all idiots. Steve, however, was different. I could immediately relate to him. Steve had experience with the differences between heroin and cocaine. Years prior, one of the dimwitted shrinks

I'd been to told me it was cleaner and healthier for me to shoot heroin than cocaine. Following the good doctor's advice, I immediately scored some heroin, proudly justifying to my friends that my doctor had told me that shooting heroin was better for me than shooting coke. Steve was young and hip. He told me stories about his own experiences with drugs. One of his favorite trips was taking psychedelics and riding his motorcycle around the mountains. Listening, I knew this guy was for real. He wasn't bullshitting me. Previous counselors, who'd never done drugs themselves, claimed books and secondhand information qualified them to advise me. It absolutely did not. Steve was the real thing. He'd been there and he knew what it was like.

I believe it takes an addict to know an addict. We are all the same. We speak the same language because of our common experiences. For that reason, I believe, we are drawn to each other like magnets. **We seek each other's company, in the disease and in recovery.**

Steve was the only counselor who got my attention. I listened, and as I listened, for the first time, I considered a life without drugs. "Wow," I wondered, "Can I stop doing blow, mushrooms, acid, and heroin?" Notice, I did not mention buds. That still hadn't occurred to me. Never in my wildest dreams did I think I would stop smoking pot. I didn't even consider marijuana a drug. To me, it was more like tobacco. Some people smoke cigarettes every day, I rationalized, I smoked pot every day. If joints were cigarettes, I'd have been a-pack-a-day smoker. By the way, I smoked cigarettes, too!

I thought it might be possible for me to stop using "real" drugs—someday. Steve encouraged me to ponder the possibility that there might be life after thirty. Prior to this conversation with him, I'd resigned myself to the notion that drugs would take me out young. I'd always considered myself a fire—burning hard and fast, enjoying it as much as possible, for as long as possible. I never believed I would make it to adulthood.

Steve didn't talk about some vague day in the future when I might give up drugs. He recommended that I check into a thirty-day drug rehabilitation center immediately. I agreed that it might be a good idea someday and told him I'd think about it and let him know. Then he stressed that by "now," he meant "tomorrow morning"—not "someday."

"You must be fucking high!" I kidded, and we both laughed. No way, I thought. If he wasn't high, then he was crazy.

Steve wasn't easily dissuaded. He pointed out that I looked like a dead man walking and he told me that he was gravely concerned that I might accidentally overdose on my birthday. I did have an extremely high tolerance, and I wasn't as physically fit as I was when I began with drugs. Because I was weaker now than I'd ever been, there was a risk that my body couldn't handle the amount I was used to giving it. I was thin, tired, and beat up from a strain of my addiction, and I was planning on hitting it hard on my birthday. I thought his concern was lame at first, but then I had to admit that it was a possibility. So I listened as Steve persuasively described the hospital.

God love him, he seriously misrepresented the hospital. He painted a picture of a Club Med where I could get into great shape and clear my head. He was definitely an addict, because he knew just what to say to hook me. I excitedly latched onto the concept of cleaning out my system, which essentially meant lowering my tolerance. A little rest and some nourishment would be bonuses, but the real motivation for me was that after thirty days clean, it would be easier to get high on less stash.

What sealed the deal was that this little break would be the perfect excuse for getting out of doing some major assignments due at school. So, for those two reasons and for Mom, I agreed to enter a drug rehabilitation program. I really had no intention of staying sober. "Someday" wasn't here yet.

CHAPTER 11
AGE 16 - 17

I checked into Coldwater Canyon Hospital on October 1, 1984, the day before my seventeenth birthday. Coldwater Canyon was a lock-down adolescent hospital for drug and alcohol abusers. On the way to the hospital, I smoked a big fat joint. Mom and Sam drove me, and I'd talked them into letting me light up on the way. I smoked another one in the parking lot before walking in. I had another one hidden in my shoe for safekeeping.

My initiation into Coldwater was a surprising strip search. They undressed me down to my boxers and thoroughly searched my luggage while I waited. They failed to earn my respect and admiration, however, when they overlooked the joint hidden underneath the sole of my shoe. I deemed them amateurs, and determined that I was not likely to be impressed or inspired by anything they had to say. At least I still had the joint.

I obligingly cooperated with orientation, but I did not dig the place at all. Eventually, I was escorted to my room, which, to my chagrin, I would be sharing with several other guys. Walking down the hallway, I noticed a couple of guys like myself who looked cool, a couple of dorks who didn't, and thankfully, a couple of cuties who perked my interest.

The first week I spent in Coldwater Canyon was a nightmare. Surprisingly, I did not suffer major physical withdrawal, but emotionally, I was in a really bad state. I was angry, and I let everyone know it. I really hated the place and the outlandish crap they were preaching. It was absurd and unreasonable that they expected me to get totally clean and sober. The counselors had to be fucking kidding. I swore they were smoking dope themselves. They were insane if they thought I was going to stay sober every day for the rest of my life. The concept was unthinkable. I was a partier—a head. I was not a dork. I was just there to take a break, clean up a little, and then get back to my life. I was not going to stop partying. Partiers partied. **If I stopped partying, then I wouldn't be the same person.**

At the end of my first week's phone restriction, I was on the phone with my mom. I was screaming at her and threatening to kill Steve if she didn't get me the hell out of there. "Tell him! You fucking tell him I am going to slit his fucking throat unless you get me the fuck out of here!"

"Please, Robbie." Mom cried, "Please, stay there for me. I've never asked you for anything, but I am asking you to do this. Please, stay for the thirty days." I cried too. I was so frustrated and alarmed at how upset she was. My emotions were all over the place. That was the first week in years that I hadn't gotten high, and **I wasn't used to feeling anything, let alone everything**. I was confused, angry, sad, and frustrated. I felt like a sissy for crying. I reluctantly agreed to stay, and in return, my mom promised me that I would not have to stay there more than thirty days.

I endured three more weeks of hell in lock-down rehabilitation. It did give me time to contemplate what it would be like to get totally clean, but in my heart, I knew I was not done yet. **I could not imagine a life without drugs and alcohol.** I was too young to get sober. What about college? If I went to college, I *had* to party there. I wouldn't know what to do with myself if I quit using. What about all my friends? How could I be around them and not get high?

The days at the hospital were long, and the sessions with therapists and patients were monotonous. I sat in group sessions all day long and occasionally met individually with the counselor assigned to my case. I resisted vehemently for the first two weeks of therapy. Then, exhausted from fighting, I wised up. I realized that if I could not dazzle them with my brilliance, then I would have to baffle them with my bullshit! And so I did, or at least I thought I did. I told them what I thought they wanted to hear. I sounded enthusiastic about sobriety and feigned excitement about leading a different kind of life. I learned all the sober language. I expressed hope for my future and all the opportunities that would open up for me if I stayed clean. A small part of me wanted to believe what I was saying—I was so good that I nearly bought my own bullshit.

I elaborated on how being exposed to sobriety and The Twelve Steps of Alcoholics Anonymous had changed my life. I lied to the group in therapy and to the counselor in my private sessions. I turned in Oscar-worthy performances so the steering committee would grant me special privileges and the counselors would believe they had reached me.

As my thirty days drew to a close, I let my guard down a little and told everyone how excited I was to get out of there. Once this news made it back to the counselors, however, they determined that if I was that anxious to leave, I must not be ready to go. I rallied to save my act by telling everyone how much I was going to miss them and that I'd come back to visit. Again, I wanted to believe what I was saying and I did think there was an outside chance I might stay sober, but I wasn't going to bet on it. What were the odds?

On day thirty, the day of my scheduled release, a counselor told me that Mom had arrived. I found her seated with every counselor from the facility. All eyes were on me. I knew it was not going to be good. The counselors gave Mom their collective opinion. They said that I was one of the sickest addicts they knew. Of the hundreds they had seen come and go; I was, categorically, among the worst. They had not arrived at this consensus lightly. They informed her that they had reached this conclusion through careful analysis and years of field experience. They strongly recommended that I stay on at Coldwater Canyon longer, making it pointedly clear to my mom that if I were to leave it would be Against Medical Advice (AMA) and that the chances of me staying sober were slim to none. Finally, they told her that if I left and my life continued on its current path there was a strong likelihood that I would eventually die from my drug and alcohol addiction.

Devastated by their estimation, she began sobbing. She appealed to whatever good sense I might have to please stay. I freaked out at first, furious to be cornered this way, but then, my survival instinct kicked in. I calmed down and played it right. I told everyone that I appreciated their concern, but that they hadn't known me long enough to make such a grim determination. I told them that I intended to channel the same energy I'd devoted to getting high into staying clean. I was dedicated to living a life of sobriety, and having been exposed to all the possibilities it offered, there was no way I would turn my back on sobriety. I had changed, I declared. My whole life had changed, and there was no way I would go back to the ugliness of using.

Once again, I was so sincere in my conviction that a part of me believed what I was saying. I would have sworn to it without hesitation. And if I didn't mean it, a part of me truly wanted to mean it. But there was another deep-seated part inside me that said "Shut the fuck up! Who cares? There is no way I will see the age of thirty. I am a drug addict, and I will always be a drug addict—so stay out of my fucking way!"

It didn't matter anyway. The therapists en masse said they wished they could believe me, but regardless of my intentions, they feared the addiction would get the better of me. They were convinced I would use again if I left the hospital after only thirty days. The decision wasn't theirs though. It was a voluntary program, and because I was still a minor, they could only keep me there with my mother's consent.

"Mom, you and I had a deal." I pulled out my ace. "Please don't let me down now. I need to know you have my back." Mom reluctantly honored her word, but she cried throughout the entire discharge process.

CHAPTER 12
AGE 17

It was incredibly difficult to return to classes at Chatsworth High. I was surprised to find that I had meant what I'd said. I did want to try to stay sober. I wasn't totally full of shit after all. My friends, however, did not have the same goal. They said they supported my sobriety, but their underlying motive was to have me back in the pit with them. After all, misery loves company. I went to parties with them, and we'd have long conversations about getting sober while they got high. They were just biding their time until they saw a way to get me using again. Addicts do not like to lose another partying buddy, especially one who could supply them with drugs.

Eventually, their partying began to wear on me, and little by little, my resolve to stay clean weakened. The first time I caved, I very carefully inhaled weed without any guilt. A friend of mine, who had also once been clean, blew pot smoke towards my mouth and nose so that I had no choice but to breathe it in. Granted, I could have held my breath, but I chose not to. The joint never touched my fingers or lips. He may have done it deliberately and intentionally, but since I did not touch the joint, it was not my fault. That was the story I told myself to justify it. Since I could say, literally, that I had not smoked pot, I still considered myself clean and sober. After I shared what happened with Steve, he perceived the situation differently and strongly suggested that I had slipped.

Despite what Steve said though, as far as I was concerned, I was still clean and sober. I stayed sober for another couple of weeks until I hooked up with a girl who was known for being easy when she was drunk. I took a bottle of liquor from Mom's liquor cabinet and set out to get her drunk and get some lovin'. It was a good plan, but I executed it poorly. I managed to get her drunk, but in the process, I also got drunk. Until that night, I had managed to stay sober for thirty days after my release from rehab—excluding the secondhand pot smoke. When I did begin using again, I was able to avoid detection for yet another thirty days, but once my mom caught on, she sent me right back to Coldwater Canyon.

I returned to the program with my tail between my legs, expecting condescension from the counselors. Instead, I received an empathetic and compassionate welcome back. Rather than gloating about successfully predicting my downfall, they wanted to know **if I was willing to do what it took to stay sober.** I was. I stayed at Coldwater Canyon Hospital and did everything that was asked of me without resistance or complaint. I finished all of the work that was assigned to me and eagerly participated in sessions just like I'd done in school before I'd ever gotten high. I really wanted sobriety this time around. There was still a whisper of doubt in my mind, but it was drowned out by the noise of constant fellowship and collaboration on our common goal—sobriety. I spent a total of four months in that thirty-day program. I became the program's veteran patient.

CHAPTER 13
AGE 17 - 18

This time, when I left Coldwater Canyon I had the support of the counselors. My therapist suggested that I live in a halfway house called Cry Help, but our insurance would not cover it and we could not afford it. So I lived at home with Mom, Sam, and Brett. I did not return to Chatsworth High. Instead, I was enrolled at Coutin, a very small, inexpensive private school in Canoga Park. This was not an exclusive, upper-class private school. In fact, to call Coutin a school at all was a stretch. The classrooms were empty shell mobile homes, and the entire school was no bigger than a 7-11 parking lot. I hated the place. It was like a kennel for dogs.

Staying sober the second time was incredibly difficult. I continued going to AA meetings, although, at that time, Alcoholics Anonymous did not have many young people enrolled. I did meet a few other teenagers trying to stay clean, and we all banded together. There was an organization called the Palmer Drug Abuse Program, or PDAP, that catered to young people staying sober, and we often attended their meetings. There was also a really fun dance every Friday night in Santa Monica. We looked forward to it all week long. Some of my best times in early sobriety were in that dance hall. It was the first time I was able to have fun being sober.

Our young sober crowd became a very close-knit group. We had a lot of fun together during a very trying time in our lives.

We supported and understood each other. Having each others' support made it easier to maintain sobriety. We hung out after meetings at Denny's Restaurant or Norm's Diner and drank coffee all night. Our motto was "Sober and Crazy." We did stupid things. We danced on tables in restaurants, drove our cars like idiots, and always defended our actions by saying, "Hey, at least we're sober!" We were too young and new to recovery to understand that **sobriety wasn't just about being physically sober—it was about living sober.** But we were doing the best we could at the time.

I did everything I could to try to convert my old friends to the sober way of life, preaching the "sober word" like gospel. I had this need to tell everyone that I was an ex-drug addict who'd gotten clean. I wanted people to know how hard-core I had been and that I had taken drug use to an entirely different level. I wasn't partying anymore, but **my self-image and my identity were still based on my reputation for partying.** I was still under the impression that I'd been cool because I was a partier and that those who didn't party were geeks. I wanted people to know I was still cool. I was a head who didn't party anymore, but I was not a dork who had never partied at all. I had bumper stickers that read "Sober and Crazy!" and "My other car is up my nose" and stickers that boasted the Trinity sign, which is the emblem for AA.

My days of sobriety continued. Mom, however, was irritated because I was either never home or home so late. She and I began arguing about me spending so much time away. We had a couple of big fights because she wouldn't let me leave the house. Finally, in an attempt to get me to stop going out so much, she took away my car.

All of my new friends lived on the Westside of LA in Santa Monica, Venice, and Hollywood. I still lived on the far north end of The Valley, nearly half an hour away *without* traffic. I spent a great deal of time commuting between my house and theirs. I was only able to get back and forth as often as I did because Dad had bought me a VW Bug before the credit card fiasco.

Brett had just turned sixteen and didn't have a car, so my mother took mine from me and gave it to him. Brett had begun partying again, which added insult to injury. He wasn't partying like I had, but still, he was getting high. I had been staying clean and sober and using the car to get back and forth to AA meetings, and Brett was getting high and driving my car. The injustice was killing me, but I'd never been a narc, and I certainly wasn't going to start by ratting on my own brother. Without transportation, though, I couldn't hang out with my sober friends as often or get to and from the meetings I wanted to attend. This was a major issue between Mom and me, and we fought continuously about it.

One of my sober friends from Venice, Richard, was kind enough to drive all the way out to Chatsworth to pick me up so that I could still attend AA and PDAP meetings with the group and hang out for coffee afterwards. He'd then drive me all the way back home again late at night. Fortunately for me, I turned eighteen just a few weeks after Mom took the car away. As soon as I did, I moved out.

I moved in with Richard and his brother at their mom's place in Venice. She had a fairly small two-bedroom apartment, but I was thrilled to be living on the side of the hill I preferred and close to all the meetings I enjoyed. My life revolved around meetings and coffee houses. It was awesome, and it inspired me to live clean and sober for five months. I had my freedom and a new lease on life. I loved everything about my new way of life except that I didn't have any cash or any wheels. In fact, I didn't have a dime to my name. I needed money for coffee at Denny's and to put gas in Richard's car. I got a job as a busboy at a Mexican restaurant in The Valley, and Richard dropped me off at the restaurant before each shift and picked me up every night. I was quite miserable in that job. It became clear to me that the car and lifestyle I had in mind for myself were not attainable on minimum wage plus tips, especially in Los Angeles.

It occurred to me that my grandmother in Miami might be willing to help me. She and I had a fabulous relationship, one that hadn't been tainted by my drug use because she hadn't been subjected to it. I called her to see if she would lend me enough money to get into an apartment with Richard. I would need my share of first and last month's rent and a security deposit, around one thousand dollars. She listened to my request and then countered with an even more appealing offer.

She suggested that I come out to Miami and live with her long enough to finish my last year of high school and get my diploma. To lure me, she said if I did, I could have the 280 ZX that used to belong to her son, my Uncle Donald. Then, as if I wasn't already convinced, she added that, after graduation, she would give me the money I wanted for the apartment. How could I turn that down? I wasn't stoned or stupid. I accepted her offer. It was the best way I had of getting both the money necessary to secure a place in LA and a car. She called me back, just minutes later, to inform me I had a reservation on a flight out of LAX at 4:30 that afternoon. My jaw dropped. How could I pick up and leave like that? But after some deliberation, I was on the plane a few hours later, leaving for Miami.

CHAPTER 14
AGE 18

Before I left for Miami, I contacted all my friends and assured them that I would go to meetings and stay sober in Miami. I vowed to return in seven months, after graduating high school, with a 280 ZX and some cash. **I was devoted to staying sober, and I'd have sworn an oath to prove it.** I landed in Miami the same determined guy I'd been when I left California: long, bleached-white hair, dangling earrings and all. Glam rock was all the rage and I'd gotten caught up in the style.

My Aunt Dawn greeted me at the airport well after midnight. Eight years my senior and also a head, she always had a joint in her mouth. The joint, however, was the least of her problems—she was addicted to cocaine. She'd had reconstructive surgery on her nose because heavy cocaine use had destroyed it, so seeing her with a joint between her lips, instead of a straw up her nose, was a definite improvement. Ironically, her problems with drugs had helped dissuade me from drug use for quite awhile when I was younger. I'd promised my mom and my grandmother that I'd never do drugs as a result of Dawn and Luis Donald's drug-related issues. Nearly a decade later, again trying to stay away from drugs, I was about to spend my time hanging out with her. This time, her drug use would facilitate my journey away from sobriety.

Once we'd retrieved my luggage from baggage claim, we hopped into Dawn's Jaguar, which was conspicuously parked in a red zone right outside of arriving flights. Even though Dawn knew I was sober, she immediately sparked up the joint she'd left resting in the ashtray, and before I'd even fastened my seatbelt, I was taking a hit myself. This was an incredibly confusing moment. It happened without any thought. I felt as though everything was in slow motion; it was a surreal dream state. I held the smoke in as Dawn pulled the car away from the curb, and then slowly let it escape. I was shocked and disappointed in myself, and at the same time, so incredibly relieved that I didn't have to worry about that decision any more.

"Ah," I said, smiling contentedly, "this is what I'm talking about! Finally, a good, righteous buzz! I needed this!" I was home. I didn't know how all my sincere convictions had literally gone up in smoke so quickly, but I felt right again for the first time in a long time. I felt like I was exactly where I belonged. **The addict inside of me had not died; he had just been napping, and now I had awakened him.**

Dawn was married to a very charismatic and sophisticated Cuban drug smuggler named Luis. He was the ultimate classy junkie. Everyone who knew him loved him. He was a fun-loving and handsome guy. Luis became my best friend and mentor the moment we hooked up. I wanted to be everything Luis was. He became my idol. My first night in Miami, I went to dinner with Luis and Dawn. While we were at the restaurant, Luis said something to her in Spanish. I found out later that he'd been asking her permission to involve me in his business. He needed help the following night picking up a big shipment of pot. After obtaining Dawn's consent, Luis disclosed the plan. A small plane would be dropping the buds off shore. A boat would pick them up and deliver them to a dock at midnight. He could use an extra set of hands, if I was interested and willing. I enthusiastically agreed to help.

The next afternoon, Dawn and I got high again. She told me

that she thought it would be a good idea if I lost the earrings and got a haircut. I told her I wasn't about to lose the earrings, but that I'd be willing to wear studs instead of dangling ones. I also agreed, albeit reluctantly, to get my hair cut, but insisted that it only needed to be trimmed. We smoked another joint on the way to the hair salon. When we arrived, the salon served us chilled champagne. By the time I was seated and ready to have my hair trimmed, I was toast. My aunt said something to the stylist in Spanish, and the next thing I knew, she was chopping my hair. It fell in long strands to the floor all around me. Apparently Dawn had told her friend to cut it all off and that is exactly what she did.

I watched, totally stoned and completely silent, as my long hair went from shoulder length to a butch cut. I was dumbfounded, tripping out, and utterly incapable of objecting. It would have been too late, anyway. When it was all done and my hair was all gone, I went into a mini-depression. *Its funny how, at that age, I put so much stock in my image. My long hair had been a large part of my perception of who I was, and I had a hard time adjusting to its absence. I felt I made a totally different impression without my long hair. I felt I had to represent something altogether different once it was gone, but I wasn't sure what that was.*

* * *

That night, Luis and I drove his Jeep to the docks where we picked up nearly five hundred pounds of marijuana—six eighty-pound bags to be exact. We arrived at the dock shortly after midnight, and we soon saw a small light on the horizon in Miami Bay. As the boat approached, I could see that the light was from a flashlight, not from any lights on the boat. The guys manning the boat were wearing helmets and infrared masks so they could see in the darkness. We watched and waited as the boat drew closer.

Standing there, on the opposite coast, miles from home, waiting to do my part in a drug smuggling operation, I couldn't believe this was my life. As soon as the boat pulled up to the shore, we got busy. Without conversation, we quickly unloaded the potato sacks of buds and heaped them onto the back of Luis' Jeep. Throwing a bag over my shoulder, I was amazed at how much things had changed in just seventy-two hours. I was living in Miami, and I'd lost my sobriety and my hair. I was hoisting an eighty-pound bag of pot over my shoulder. Just days ago, in Los Angeles, I'd sworn I would never touch weed again.

Once we'd transferred the buds from the boat to the Jeep, we drove to one of Dawn and Luis's condominiums to lay the wet buds out to dry. The entire floor of this vacant condo was covered with huge sticks of weed. It was a pot smoker's dream.

CHAPTER 15
AGE 18

I had started a new chapter in my life, playing another corrupt character in another insidious setting. Although I was living with my grandmother and her husband, I spent most of my time with my aunt and uncle. I'd moved to Miami, coincidentally, just as the hit television series *Miami Vice* was becoming popular. Always quick to adapt, I readily adopted the look of the street savvy vice cops who were soaring in the television ratings.

I wore light-colored suits with bright t-shirts and meshed loafers without socks. I incorporated Latin drug smuggler panache by wearing several big gold chains around my neck, rings—even a pinky ring, and an ostentatious diamond stud earring. I carried a handgun to complete my new image, though I kept it either inside my jacket or hidden in my car. It is a miracle that I didn't get myself killed waving that gun around. Anyone watching *Miami Vice* would have assumed the show's writers were overstating the crime scene in Miami, but I knew better now. I witnessed some of the unlawful action myself. My first week in Miami, a shipment of automatic weapons was smuggled into the city and resulted in an overflow of dead bodies in the city morgues. News broadcasters reported that a fast food chain had donated freezer storage units to the city to house the additional corpses. A lot of the crime and corruption was reported in the news, but I was also getting the inside scoop from Uncle Luis.

My grandmother enrolled me at Miami Shores Preparatory School on Biscayne Boulevard. This school was as corrupt as the city. Almost all the students were Cuban, Colombian, Puerto Rican, or from New York, and when I began noticing the kinds of cars and limos they arrived to school in, I asked what their parents did for a living. The standard answer was, "They are in the business." By this, they meant the cocaine business. It was shocking. I was so used to dealers hiding what they did that it was bizarre to be somewhere it was commonplace. In Miami, at that time, saying you were in the cocaine business was like folks in Hollywood saying they were in the entertainment business. It was no big deal.

On the first day of school, I met up with the school's heads, the partiers. A girl named Heather asked me if I wanted to go smoke a joint with her and her friends. I joined them and Heather ended up being my girlfriend for most of my stay in Miami. Heather loved smoking pot, but she hated everything else—especially blow. My return to cocaine use undeniably got in the way of our relationship.

When I began using cocaine again, my time at Coldwater Canyon began to haunt me. I felt guilty and confused about losing my sobriety. **A head full of recovery and a body full of drugs is a terrible mix.** I kept trying to convince myself that I could tame the beast of addiction and just party like a "normal" person. I rationalized that since I wasn't slamming blow, I wasn't as bad as I had been before treatment. **It is amazing how cunning and baffling addiction can be. I knew I was a drug addict and an alcoholic, but I was convinced I could be the exception to the rule, and I kept trying to prove it.** I was not like everyone else I knew who was suffering from drug addiction. I was going to be the one who was strong enough to beat it, smart enough to fool it, and determined enough to thwart it.

While attending Miami Shores Prep, I met a guy named Sean,

and we started hanging out together. He was from New York and, according to Luis' information, from an Italian mafia family. Sean and I got into a lot of trouble together. We ditched school and partied every day. It didn't take us long to find out where all the crack houses were, and it took us even less time to find out who was running them. We copped rock steadily from one place or another.

I had to go to crack houses because Dawn and Luis were not being as generous with their blow as I'd expected, especially not when I intended to take it elsewhere. I wanted some to do with my friends, and that didn't fly with them. Luis and Dawn always had pot around, and I'd smoke weed with them all day long. Blow, however, was a different story. We did that less frequently, but when we did, it was always an all-nighter. On one such occasion, after being up all night, we stopped late in the morning and went to bed. Later that day, around 3:30 p.m., my school called to inquire about my day's absence. Luis answered the phone and screamed at the principal, "Never call this house this early again!"

The other friend I met at school was named Jorge. He was from Colombia, and his father was also "in the business." He was a very nice guy, unlike Sean. Sean might have been cool, but he was also a criminal. Jorge was not. He was a solid guy, who, unfortunately, hooked up with the wrong guy—me. He spent a lot of time with me, and, therefore, smoked a lot of rock. It wasn't long before Jorge was hooked on crack, too. Then there was this Puerto Rican kid named Jimmy, whose reputation preceded him. He was bad news. I'd heard all sorts of horrible stories about him, like how he'd shot this guy at a party, almost got busted breaking into a car, or killed a guy the other night. I was stunned by the stories I'd heard and asked Heather how it was that this guy hadn't been busted. People were obviously aware of who was pulling this shit, yet Jimmy kept getting away with it. Heather explained that Jimmy's dad happened to be a top ranking cop with the Miami

Police Department—and a dirty cop at that. She begged me not to befriend Jimmy, claiming it would only get me into trouble or get me killed.

When I finally fell in with Jimmy, it was entirely by mistake. I had generated all kinds of problems for myself at school by cutting classes and getting caught smoking dope. I always arrived late in the morning and came back late after lunch. The school also did not appreciate the verbal onslaughts they received from Luis each time they called "too early." Still, the school tolerated all of this for awhile. It took a prize-winning deviant act to finally get me kicked out. I got into an argument with Principal Dr. Klar in his office. In front of my grandmother, I became so enraged that I called Dr. Klar a fucking dick. Then I stood up, leaned across his desk, and spit in his face. That did it. He expelled me.

My grandmother met with Dr. Klar to negotiate my continued enrollment at Miami Shores Preparatory High School. It cost her ten thousand dollars and required my presence in Dr. Klar's office or an empty classroom, from 3:00 to 4:00 p.m., Monday through Friday, after everyone else had left campus. I would have to take one class per day, for one hour of the day, rather than the five classes a day I was accustomed to taking. It was called "Dr. Klar's After School Plan." It was an interesting deal for all involved, but I wasn't complaining. My schedule had just gotten a whole lot lighter.

There was one other student on Dr. Klar's plan. Her name was Tammy and she was Heather's best friend and Jimmy's girlfriend. Tammy and I had a totally platonic relationship. She and I would get together every day and hang out smoking pot and drinking on the deck at my grandmother's home overlooking the bay. Heather was always a little jealous and suspicious, but she never made a big deal out of it. Jimmy, on the other hand, did. He found out I was hanging out with Tammy and was convinced I was sleeping with her. Therefore, he was going to have to kill me.

Considering Jimmy's infamy, I really didn't like hearing that I was on his hit list. Heather didn't either. She was really freaked out and certain that if I didn't get out of town quickly I'd be dead—and she told my grandmother as much. My grandma, however, was not too distressed and seemed certain Jimmy was all talk.

Tammy kept assuring Jimmy things were fine, that I was cool and that nothing had ever happened between us, but he wasn't hearing her. Soon she, too, feared for my life.

Then one day Jimmy called me at my grandmother's house. Heather was there with me at the time. Jimmy was livid. He was out of his mind, screaming at me over the phone, "You motherfucker, come meet me and deal with this like a man!" I couldn't get a word in edgewise. Jimmy kept pummeling me with threats and all the while Tammy was in the background pleading with him to let this alone, insisting she and I were just friends. Heather knew Jimmy fairly well so she tried to pacify Jimmy directly, but to no avail. Jimmy was completely berserk. He kept seething, threatening to stalk me down and kill me, either on the street or in my sleep.

Tammy, out of frustration or desperation, wrenched the phone away from Jimmy in the midst of all this and hung it up. Heather and I seized the opportunity to seek my grandmother's assistance, telling her the seriousness of the situation and imploring her to help me get out of town. Astoundingly, my grandma still refused to acknowledge that I was in any danger. Instead, she wanted to talk to Jimmy the next time he called. She was sure that she could calm him down and put an end to this craziness once and for all. Heather and I laughed at the absurdity of her suggestion, but conceded with the stipulation that if she failed, she'd put me on the next flight to Los Angeles.

Heather and I went back to my room and started packing. She was crying because I was leaving, and I was sad, too, although I was relieved and very grateful to be getting out of this situation and out of Miami. We heard the phone ringing some minutes later, and assumed it was Jimmy calling back. My grandmother answered the call, but we couldn't hear what she was saying. Heather went out to the living room so that she could listen to at least one side of the conversation, but I didn't bother.

"You aren't going to believe this," she said returning to my room, "She's speaking calmly with Jimmy." I looked up from what I was doing in disbelief, my jaw dropped in astonishment. I followed Heather back out to the other room where we caught the tail end of the conversation, "Jimmy, of course I would be honored to attend your and Tammy's wedding." Stunned, we stared as they said their goodbyes and then my grandmother told Jimmy she'd put me back on the phone. I didn't know what to do. I took the phone and tentatively said, "Hello?"

"Hey," Jimmy said, "You have a really cool grandmother. I'm really sorry for all this." I couldn't believe what I was hearing; not only was he being cool, he'd actually just apologized. Somehow before the call ended, I'd agreed to get together with him and smoke a joint. Sure enough, about an hour later the four of us were together getting high.

Jimmy and I became very good friends in spite of our rocky beginning. After that situation had worked itself out, we became partners in crime. We actually had the audacity to hit a crack house. We dealt a lot of cocaine and we smoked a lot of cocaine. Jimmy and I were good together, or bad together, depending on how you look at it.

On more than one occasion, Jimmy joyfully recalled the story of how much he hated me before we became friends. Jimmy laughed each time he told the story; he would wait all night outside of my grandmother's house ready to put a bullet in my head. Fortunately for me, he picked nights that I did not go home. Whenever he reminisced I was not amused and usually just remained silent. Jimmy and I spent a lot of time together. Young and bold, we pushed the limits with our unlawful behavior.

My time with Jimmy started coming to an end when I kept stalling our plan to rob another blow dealer. We knew this dealer was receiving a shipment of fourteen to fifteen kilos of cocaine. The only contingency was that since this guy's mother lived with him, there was a good possibility that she would be at the house when we were going to do the hit. Jimmy made it very clear that, if needed, I had to be willing to kill her.

We staked out the dealer's house, driving by several times a day to monitor his schedule. His shipment arrived, but I kept finding excuses to delay the robbery. Jimmy got pissed and called me a coward. Each time he called me gutless, I retaliated, "I'll do the hit! Will you just chill!" Tormented, I hesitated. I wanted to steal the blow, but I wasn't a killer.

Any decent person would not have even considered murdering that woman. While I wasn't decent, thankfully I was not coldhearted enough to go through with it. I resolved that I would rather deal with Jimmy's temper than the alternative. He was livid when I finally told him. After that, Jimmy and I did not hang out much. I was embarrassed because he thought I was being weak. It was a compromise that I was more than willing to accept.

CHAPTER 16
AGE 18

I was driving the 280 ZX that my grandmother had offered me, though it wasn't officially mine yet. She'd promised me the car after I graduated high school, but she made it available to me when I'd arrived in Miami. That car made hundreds of drug runs and served as our mobile drug room. I'd managed to obtain an enormous industrial torch that we used for hitting the pipe. We'd drive up and down Biscayne or Collins Boulevard, and when we stopped at a red light, I'd lean my seat back, light the torch, and take a hit while Jimmy, Sean, or Jorge watched for the light to turn green. Once the light changed, I'd raise my seat, hand off the torch, and let out a huge base hit that would fill the whole car with a thick cloud of smoke. I'd start to drive at five miles an hour, not accelerating much faster until the rush subsided enough for me to gather my senses. Once the whirring in my ears stopped and my eyes could almost focus, off we'd go, smoke billowing out the windows.

Months went by in a haze of one crazy escapade after another. Our drug life became routine. I was either smoking rock with my friends or smoking pot with Dawn and Luis. Usually when I was with Luis and Dawn, it meant we were going on a drug run. Luis used to take me out to various ranches in Homestead, Florida where he'd introduce me to one drug lord or another. These guys lived on huge, sprawling estates surrounded by impenetrable walls and security gates with surveillance cameras and watchtowers manned by armed snipers. My uncle pointed out the guard towers when we visited an estate. Driving in, we knew there were rifles trained on us. I was so impressed with this lifestyle that I thought I might strive to achieve it for myself someday.

On one such excursion, I met a Cuban drug lord who didn't speak much English. However, in English, he made a comment I liked. He nodded toward me and said to Luis, "I like this kid. I can see him running your family business some day." That was exactly what I wanted to hear! On that run, there was so much cocaine in the room with us that I could barely keep my jaw closed. This meeting took place in an empty apartment in a complex this guy was building. One of the walls in the apartment was literally stacked floor to ceiling with kilos of cocaine. There must have been three to four hundred packs. I was totally *blown* away by the sight of so much *blow*! I didn't let it show. We left with a few kilos for our buyer, Doug.

Doug was one of Luis' buyers from Naples. He was a mountain of a man who liked to get high and pop Quaaludes. Luis, Dawn, and I would spend a couple of nights entertaining Doug each time he came to town. Each meeting with him involved at least two days of partying, in addition to conducting the business at hand. My aunt and uncle always made sure they had enough Quaaludes, or at least generic "ludes," on hand before he arrived. We were really good at making sure our guests had a good time.

On one of Doug's trips over from Naples, Luis and I took him to a little motel to party. This motel was not one of our usual haunts and was unlike most of our partying locales. Luis warned me before we checked in to stay cool if we happened to smoke any rock with Doug. He did not want me to appear at all apprehensive in case Doug might sense it and become suspicious of the deal. Luis' concern was not unwarranted. To everyone's annoyance, including my own, I became a paranoid freak whenever I did blow. I was a nightmare to be around. This hadn't always been the case. I didn't react that way to cocaine until after I had started shooting it. Once I'd slammed it, it no longer mattered how I took it; I became delusional every time. I heard noises and saw things. Eventually cocaine use made me so skittish that my friends nicknamed me "Sketch." Apparently Doug, too, was known for his propensity for paranoia when he did blow. That was the last thing we needed: a loaded, anxious and irrationally suspicious out-of-town buyer.

Despite forewarnings from Luis, I started hearing noises while partying at the motel. I did everything I could to control myself, but I kept hearing noises at the front door. It was like trying not to sneeze when your nose tickles. I would take a hit and then walk to the bathroom so that I could walk past the front door of the room and listen intently for whatever I could hear outside. Each time I walked by, I was sure I heard something just outside the door. It was killing me not to look, but Luis was already giving me dirty looks.

Doug had already noticed my behavior, though, and handed me the opportunity I wanted. He asked me what I'd heard, and then, once I told him, he told me to check it out. I gratefully looked out the peephole on the door, expecting to see the usual nothing and got the surprise of my life. Right there, on the other side of the door, someone else also had their eye to the peephole! My breath caught and I swear my heart stopped. I stepped away from the door and said, with much more composure than I felt, "Somebody is right outside!"

Luis, disgusted, walked across the room to the door and said, "Goddamn it, you guys, there is nobody there!" He flung the door wide open as he finished his declaration. Two men in business suits with walkie-talkies were standing right outside our door. They were as startled as we were. For an instant, we all just looked at each other—stunned.

"Excuse us," the suit closest to us finally said, with a nervous edge in his voice. "We did not mean to disturb you." They turned and walked away. Luis shut the door and turned around to look at us. He was freaked out. We quickly loaded the few packs of blow we had out into a duffle bag and slipped out the back window of the motel room. We made it to our car and left, still in shocked silence, expecting to see the cops behind us any second, but we never did. This incident, however, completely affirmed my paranoia for the rest of my partying days.

* * *

Luis and I would also cop heroin in the projects, where Luis was "the man" and considered the big dope dealer. He supplied the tenants there with the blow they used for crack. They, in turn, provided him with heroin whenever he wanted it—guaranteed. Whenever we showed up there, regardless of the time, which was usually three or four in the morning, everyone there bent over backwards to make us happy. The residents there catered to our every whim; whatever we wanted, we got. The place was disgusting and wonderful. It was a sure thing and a safe haven at any hour. The site might have been deplorable, but we knew it was a sanctuary.

The last time I ever slammed heroin, I was in the projects with Luis, and we scored some pure heroin called "China White" and slammed it in a bathroom. Luis poked himself between his toes so his wife, my Aunt Dawn, wouldn't see any marks. She always checked him for marks. I, however, just stuck myself in the arm.

This stuff knocked me out and over, literally. Within seconds of poking myself, I was hit hard with a warm rush that knocked me backwards into the bathtub. I lay there for some time before Luis was able to get me up and out of there. I was having trouble walking and could barely stand. I stumbled into a guy and he pulled a knife on me. He'd have stabbed me if he hadn't recognized my Uncle Luis.

I was so nauseated from this hit that Luis had to pull over several times for me to throw up. He finally got me to a 7-Eleven where I bought some orange juice and a candy bar to get my blood sugar up. This helped me salvage the high, and about a half an hour later, I was able to actually enjoy myself. I'll never forget though how close I came to death that night.

CHAPTER 17
AGE 18

Drug use took me to some sleazy places. It's inevitable. Drugs are ugly, and they come from ugly places. I went wherever I had to go to get my drugs and to get high. I would duck into any restroom, garage, or alley—no matter how grungy or shoddy—to get a fix. I hung out with some unsavory characters for the same reasons. **I had long abandoned common sense and decency at this point in my addiction. Even fear had fallen by the wayside; depression had supplanted it.** These low moments are part of the high cost of keeping up with an addiction. I had to go low to get high. Yet, there were also times I found myself partying in limos, backstage at concerts, or in VIP rooms at clubs. **These "high points" were enough of a distraction to keep me from thinking that my addiction was killing me.** Because there were times when I looked cool and together, hanging with the "right crowd," I rationalized that my addiction had not beaten me.

I continued to prove that I was willing to go to any lengths to get high. One night, Brett and our two friends, Al and Adam, visited from California. It was about three in the morning, and we had smoked the last of our rock. Everyone I knew had closed shop for the night, so coming up with more wasn't going to be easy, especially since we were not with Luis. I might have been done for the night if I hadn't been "entertaining" friends. I'd exhausted every other source, so I decided to venture into the projects and talked my friends into going with me. We set out for a place I'd heard of called Saxon. Saxon was a closed, rundown motel turned crack house.

On the drive there, I was hyper alert. My eyes were riveted to the rearview mirror, and I kept an eye out for traps ahead. Whacked out driving is a skill that we crack masters and dope fiends acquire out of necessity and paranoia. It was insane, really, how I could be paranoid enough to believe that there were bugs planted in my car, on people, or everywhere we went, but I believed that I was constantly under surveillance. Yet I was still brazen enough to attempt to score at a crack house, unannounced, in the middle of the night!

We stood out like sore thumbs during this pickup. There are not many alibis for four white guys with dilated pupils driving around the projects at that time of night. As we approached Saxon, we saw police lights ahead. Someone had been pulled over, and it appeared that they were getting busted. Immediately, we all freaked. "Oh, fuck! Get out of here!" someone yelled from the backseat. Retreat would have been the logical thing to do, but I was on a mission. **Logic was not accessible to me; I was going to score and nothing was going to stop me!** My friends, however, while they wanted me to succeed, also feared for our safety. The frenzied energy in the confined space of my 280 ZX, with voices escalating and pulses racing, was maddening.

"Shut the fuck up!" I finally ordered, pausing the craziness. "Everything is going to be all right. This will work." I pulled into the parking lot of the desolate motel and told the guys to wait for five minutes. If I did not come out in within five minutes, then they could leave. They continued to voice their protests, insisting we should leave. They pleaded with me as if they would never see me again. I knew how risky this score was, but I needed more. I was "jonesing" big time. Fear and consequences fell by the wayside.

I got out of the car and approached the closest motel room door, knocking without hesitation. The door opened just a crack. No one was visible in the doorway, so I slipped inside, again without much forethought. Just as I cleared the doorway, the door slammed shut behind me. There was a gun to my head. "What the fuck are you doing here, white boy?" the guy who'd been standing behind the door demanded, as he pressed the cold barrel of the gun against the side of my head. "Who do you know?"

A little alarmed, but totally composed, I started naming off all the crack dealers that I knew in that neighborhood—"Fat Boy, Chief, and Shaky."

"Okay," he barked. "What do you want?"

"A fifty piece," I answered, meaning I had fifty dollars.

"Give me your money," he ordered. "I'll be right back." He took my money and disappeared. Ordinarily, I'd never hand over my money up front, but these weren't ordinary circumstances. He hadn't given me another choice. I thought for sure that was the last I'd see of him and my money.

Once the guy with the gun and my money were gone, I looked around the motel room and noticed for the first time that there were other people in the room. There was a woman curled up in the corner, hugging her bony knees and staring at me. She looked like she was sixty years old. She was skin and bones. Her black skin was wrinkled like a prune, stark against her salt-and-pepper hair. She was the most memorable because of the look on her face. She stared at me with an expression of awe and fear, like a scared little girl, though she was clearly much older. There was also a man and a young girl hitting a pipe. They were totally oblivious to my presence, just fixated on the hit in the pipe. I watched them with envy. I heard the sizzle of melting rock, watched the flame of the torch as it played against the glass bowl and stem of the pipe as they twirled it steadily, and finally, I could smell the sweet odor of the smoke as the man exhaled the hit in a thick cotton candy cloud. I watched the billowing smoke float then sink to the floor. I ached. I wanted that hit so bad I could taste it. I started thinking about how I could convince those two to give me a hit if my guy didn't come back with my fifty piece. The last person I noticed was a woman sleeping on the bed. I wondered how she could possibly sleep with so much going on around her, and then decided it was because, by the looks of her, she'd been hitting it pretty hard.

Then, just like that, the guy who'd answered the door returned. I could hardly believe he'd actually come back, and to my astonishment, he'd brought a huge fifty piece for me. He wanted me to stay and hit it with him, but I told him I had someone waiting for me. His eyes widened like I'd just given him some shocking news and he yelled, "Then get the fuck out of here!"

I half walked, half ran back to the car, hoping my brother and friends were still there, and that the police weren't with them. To my relief, the car was there, and there weren't any cop cars in sight. When I opened the door, they all begged me to get the hell out of there. None of them even asked if I had been successful. Once we were a safe distance from Saxon and the projects and we were sure the police hadn't followed us, I heard a tentative, yet eager voice ask, "So, did you score?"

"What do you think?" I asked with mischievous pride. "Of course I scored! And a good piece, too!" I bragged. Brett, Adam, and Al unanimously saluted me as the craziest motherfucker they'd ever known, and they loved me for it.

CHAPTER 18
AGE 18

My time in Miami was drawing to a close, and I was setting myself up to be evicted. The first mistake I made was stealing my step-grandfather's medical bag, which contained prescription drugs and blank prescription pads. I traded Luis the blank scrips for a bag of blow and shared the narcotics with him. When my step-grandfather accused me of stealing the bag, I categorically denied it and called him a crazy old man.

Days later, my Aunt Debbie (my Uncle Donald's wife), who also happened to be the nurse who worked for my step-grandfather, called both my grandmother and my Aunt Dawn and told them that they knew for certain that I had taken the medical bag. The pharmacist had informed her that someone fitting my description had tried to fill a prescription for Valium. Aunt Debbie gave me an ultimatum. She said that if I didn't admit to stealing the medical bag and give it and all the meds back, she would report the theft to the police. With the pharmacist willing to identify me as the guy who'd tried to fill the prescription, I could have gone down for a felony. I admitted to taking the bag. My grandmother threw me out of the house and took back the 280 ZX. I got the doctor's bag back from Luis and returned it, along with what was left of the pills and prescription pads, though I never told them that I'd shared the drugs with Luis. I never narced on my partners. Never.

I moved in with Dawn and Luis, although we weren't getting along very well at that point. I knew that Dawn loved me, but she was upset with me because, as unbelievable as it seemed, she thought I was a bad influence on Luis. A few more days passed before Luis told me he'd been able to fill one of the scrips. So he and I got high and went down to the projects to score. He scored his brown, and I got whacked out on crack. When we got back to his house, my aunt freaked. She knew Luis was high on brown and blamed me for it. So she threw me out of her house, too, after she threw a half dozen full wine bottles at me. I was homeless. Luis really pissed me off at that point, because he never stepped in to help me. While I didn't have so much as a doghouse to crawl into, he acted like a bad puppy, wagging his tail and slobbering his profuse apologies all over his master—Dawn.

I spent the first night with Heather, even though she and I were on the outs and her mom didn't like me. The second night, with no place to call home, I slept under a bridge at Hallover. Desperate and wanting nothing more than to go home, I called Mom for help. I asked for a plane ticket back to California—only a ticket, nothing more. I would rather have been homeless in LA than Miami. Mom refused. She was done with me. Both my grandmother and Dawn refused me the same request.

At my wit's end, I wound up back on Dawn's doorstep. I begged her to let me move back in, but she wouldn't relent. She did, however, agree to let me take a shower, which sounded like a good idea at first. When I got out of the shower, my watch and the small bag of buds I had left were not where I'd put them. When I asked her about it, she responded matter-of-factly that she'd taken my watch because people living on the streets didn't need to know what time it was and that she'd taken my weed because I had a drug problem. I was almost in tears.

Frustrated, I asked if I could go upstairs to my old room and change into some clean clothes. She said fine, knowing all along that it wouldn't be possible. She had taken a butcher knife to all of my clothes. It was devastating. Everything was sliced and shredded. It was really a sick sight to see. Somehow, despite the disarray of everything, I noticed that some of my clothes were missing, so I asked my aunt where they were, hoping there might be something left to salvage. No such luck. Dawn haughtily directed me to look out the window. The rest of my clothes were floating in the bay. Ushering me down the stairs and out the door before I could even react, she told me to get the fuck out of there. The shower hardly seemed worth it after all that. I'd gotten cleaned up and cleaned out!

I walked the streets for a while and eventually came to rest on a bench. I watched traffic, and I noticed a man driving a pickup truck. He had two boys with him; they appeared to be his sons. From the looks of it, this man was a gardener and he was out working with his boys. I looked at that man with such envy, thinking, "Wow, this honest, working man has kids, a job, a truck, and a life." At that moment, I wanted his life so badly.

Walking the streets, having no idea where to go was one of the most miserable and sad experiences of my life! Having no money, drugs, or food in my empty stomach made it even worse!

Finally, I decided to call Uncle Donald, even though it was his wife, Debbie, who'd pulled the rug out from under me in the first place. Once I had him on the phone, I told him that his sister had just destroyed my entire wardrobe, stolen my watch, and the last of my weed, and then kicked me to the curb. He and Dawn had a love-hate relationship, and so, Donald actually believed me and empathized. Furthermore, he did not like Luis. He felt sorry for me and offered to come pick me up.

I stayed with Donald and Debbie for the next few days. It was a little awkward at first because Debbie had just busted me for stealing the medical bag. Luckily, Donald smoked pot—a lot of pot. So he and I just chilled for a few days and smoked while we discussed how I was going to get off drugs and get my life together. It was unreal.

We spent one of those lazy afternoons out on the water in Donald's boat when Dawn happened to call Donald, unaware that I was with him, frantic about a break-in and theft at home. She insisted I was the perpetrator. She claimed I'd stolen her diamond ring and earrings. Donald asked her more than once, "Are you absolutely sure it was Robbie?" She assured him that she was. She said she'd seen me face to face, literally caught me in the act.

"You're positive?" Donald asked again. He verified her story several times before letting her know he found it incredibly difficult to believe. "Well, that is really interesting," he told her, "because Robbie is right here with me and unless he swam a mile to shore, ran home and was able to get back again while I was peeing, I think you are mistaken." Dawn immediately hung up the phone. What could she say?

"I told you she was fucking nuts!" I said. This occurrence gave me some leverage. Dawn's blatant lie destroyed her credibility. Whatever feelings she may have voiced about me were tainted. The lie gave more credence to my insistence that I was a hapless victim of her insanity. I gained my family's sympathy, and thus, they became more tolerant of me. I was back in Donald and Debbie's good graces, and more importantly, I was able to regain my grandmother's support. Since her husband would have nothing to do with me, she made arrangements for me to live with a friend of hers. I don't remember much about my time there. In fact, the rest of my time in Miami is very blurry, right up until the end. I remember the end very clearly.

I was at the house my grandmother had lined up for me when Donald called, obviously upset. He sounded panicked. He told me to stay put and that he'd be right over. When he arrived, he told me how lucky I'd been that he was the only one at my grandma's house when the Miami Beach, North Miami, and Dade County Sheriff's Departments all screeched up the drive and pounded on the door looking for me. Donald insisted, as we hustled out the door, "We have to get you out of here—and out of Miami!" He bought me a plane ticket back to Los Angeles and, just hours after he'd called, watched me board a flight back to California. So just as quickly as I'd moved to Miami, I fled the city.

Later, federal agents busted Luis and Dawn for drug smuggling. The Feds had Luis on surveillance tape. He was screwed. Luis spent ten years in prison, but Dawn didn't do any time. I have to give Luis credit for that. He stepped up and was accountable for their business, not allowing Dawn any culpability at all. After they were busted, Dawn moved far out of the country and has never moved back.

CHAPTER 19

AGE 19

Once I was back in LA, my mom reluctantly agreed to take me into her home. She and Sam were still living in Chatsworth. They had a three-story townhouse, and I was given a bedroom in the basement. There was one window about six feet from the floor that was right at street level and had bars across it. It was kind of like a dungeon. My reputation as a big-time drug dealer had preceded me. Al, Adam, and Brett had shared their impressions of my situation in Miami with their friends when they returned from visiting me. So everyone had heard all about how much blow I was moving and doing and all about the Miami drug scene. Once I was back, this advanced reputation helped push me up the ladder of the drug-dealing chain in LA. My reputation helped establish me in the drug hierarchy there, although my status was never higher than it was in Miami.

My drug use was as bad as it had ever been. I continued to smoke lots of rock, although I no longer purchased it in crack form, as I'd done in Miami. I had to cook it up myself now that I was back in LA. Naturally, I became a master of cooking cocaine. Friends called me "Chef" because of how well I could cook up rock for freebasing. I still hadn't gotten rid of the nickname "Sketch," however. I was not even able to talk to people when I was on cocaine. I would just stare out windows or look for shadows under doors, always on the lookout for movement where there shouldn't be any. I could enjoy the first quarter gram or so, but after that, I was on guard duty. I slipped into another world—one of cocaine psychosis. I had delusions about cops staking me out and busting me or of creeps breaking in, ripping me off, and killing me. I thought up conspiracy theories. I had auditory and visual hallucinations. I scrutinized dirty ashtrays for microphone bugs. I examined sink faucets for cameras and checked underneath couches and car seats—looking for God knows what. I did this over and over again, even after I had just completed a thorough search. **I couldn't control myself. It was horrible each and every time I did cocaine, but I had no choice. I relived the insanity each time.**

During my drug use, I also witnessed the insanity in others. They had just started out doing drugs "only at parties" and eventually became total drug addicts. I was partying with some people one night, and this guy started crying and begging me to sell him a half-gram, fifty dollars worth, in exchange for the pink slip to his brand new Mustang. He was literally chasing me around the house, banging on doors that I had locked between us in an effort to ward him off. He was absolutely out of control. If he'd had a gun, he would have shot me to get more blow. This was a guy who'd never done cocaine before that night. It was just one example of the depravity cocaine can cause, in some, almost instantly.

I witnessed girls who would do anything, *anything*, to get just one more hit. I believe the only reason I did not take advantage of these girls was because I was too whacked out and paranoid from all the blow I was doing. However, just about every male friend of mine, and certainly most dealers, would take full advantage of the opportunity for sex tricks from these desperate girls. They'd have them do sex acts for themselves and their friends in exchange for drugs. Sometimes they'd have them do sex acts with groups of people in front of groups of people and so on—all in exchange for more cocaine. Most of these girls were "good girls" too. They were the cheerleaders and honor students who totally changed when they did blow.

This poem started circulating the Internet and anti-drug community in 2005. The author's name is unknown, but he obviously grasps the horrors of drug addiction and in particular, the nightmare that is crystal meth. This profound poem is called, "My Name is 'Meth.'"

> I destroy homes, I tear families apart,
> Take your children, and that's just the start.
> I'm more costly than diamonds, more precious than gold,
> The sorrow I bring is a sight to behold.
>
> If you need me, remember I'm easily found,
> I live all around – in schools and in town.
> I live with the rich, I live with the poor,
> I live down the street, and maybe next door.
>
> I'm made in a lab, but not like you think,
> I can be made under the kitchen sink,
> In your child's closet, and even in the woods.
> If this scares you to death, well it certainly should.
>
> I have many names, but there's one you know best,
> I'm sure you've heard of me, my name is crystal meth.
> My power is awesome, try me you'll see,
> But if you do, you may never break free.
>
> Just try me once and I might let you go,
> But try me twice, and I'll own your soul.
> When I possess you, you'll steal and you'll lie,
> You do what you have to – just to get high.

The crimes you'll commit for my narcotic charm
Will be worth the pleasure you'll feel in your arms.
You'll lie to your mother, you'll steal from your dad.
When you see their tears, you should feel sad.

But you'll forget your morals and how you were raised,
I'll be your conscience, I'll teach you my ways.
I take kids from parents, and parents from kids,
I turn people from God, and separate friends.

I'll take everything from you, your looks and your pride,
I'll be with you always – right by your side.
You'll give up everything – your family, your home,
Your friends, your money, then you'll be alone.

I'll take and take, till you have nothing more to give.
When I'm finished with you, you'll be lucky to live.
If you try me be warned – this is no game,
If given the chance, I'll drive you insane.

I'll ravish your body, I'll control your mind,
I'll own you completely, your soul will be mine.
The nightmares I'll give you while lying in bed,
The voices you'll hear from inside your head,

The sweats, the shakes, the visions you'll see,
I want you to know these are all gifts from me.
But then it's too late, and you'll know in your heart,
That you are mine, and we shall not part.

You'll regret that you tried me, they always do,
But you came to me, not I to you.
You knew this would happen, many times you were told,
But you challenged my power, and chose to be bold.

You could have said no, and just walked away,
If you could live that day over, now what would you say?
I'll be your master, you will be my slave,
I'll even go with you when you go to your grave.

Now that you have met me, what will you do?
Will you try me or not? It's all up to you.
I can bring you more misery than words can tell,
Come take my hand, let me lead you to hell.

This descriptive and poignant poem strikes at the very core of addiction.

* * *

I continued selling drugs from the basement of the townhouse. For the most part, Mom and Sam tried to remain in denial about my continued drug use and about the fact that I was dealing out of their house. I assume they just did not know what to do with me. Both of them caught me making drug deals on several occasions, either by overhearing phone calls or by witnessing meetings in the alley outside the kitchen window. They threatened to kick me out many times, but they never did. Mom also found all the stolen goods people had given me in exchange for drugs. She was upset, of course, but I never had to face any real consequences for it.

I hawked my stuff to other dealers when I ran out of drugs. I was the dealer you'd find on one day with several ounces of blow and rooms at several motels for conducting business and, on another day, walking the streets with nowhere to go and not a dime in my pocket. I lived between those extremes.

My mom also found all the guns I had under my bed. The craziness that took place while I lived there still blows me away. The drug deals, the number of people I snuck in and out, the parties I threw while they were away, and the amount of drugs that passed through that house was insane. The amount of stolen goods and guns that I had stored in my room was unbelievable. To this day, I am amazed.

One of the craziest things that ever happened while I was living at my mom's house went down when I was alone and totally whacked out on blow. I was so paranoid that someone was in the house and that others were outside breaking in that I called the cops to investigate. It was about four in the morning when I called. When they arrived at dawn, I was sweating bullets and must have looked totally out of my mind. Somehow, I managed to avoid being arrested on the spot.

Another time, I was partying with two friends of mine in my basement room. I was in a state of hysterical paranoia from smoking excessive amounts of rock, and the only way I was able to continue partying was with the assistance of my buddies. One of them, Johnny, held the pipe to my mouth, the other, whose name I can't remember, held the torch to the pipe, and all I had to do was inhale. My hands were otherwise occupied. I had a semi-automatic in one hand and a sawed off shotgun in the other. My eyes were trained on the window. I was keenly alert, primed and ready to shoot at the first sign of any passersby.

My crazy behavior was driving Johnny and the other guy nuts. Somehow, and it must have taken some clever persuasion, they managed to talk me into going to party at another friend's apartment. We were halfway there before I noticed that I hadn't changed into street clothes. No thanks to my friends, I was still wearing my boxer shorts, robe, and slippers. People at the party stared when we reached our friend's apartment. I knew some of the people there and others were strangers, but they were all dealers and thieves. The apartment was full of stolen goods, which added to my paranoia, but it did not deter me from partying.

After hitting the pipe all night, I finally crashed. I woke up to the sound of this guy, Danny, vacuuming. He said, "Get out of here. The landlord is coming in a few hours." I looked around the room, searching for Johnny and the other guy who had come with me, but they had left me. Danny continued, "No one's here, man. Everyone else left." It was late evening by then. I'd crashed from five in the morning until eight that night. Once I was fully awake, I looked around the apartment and noticed it was totally cleared out. There was nothing left in the room but the couch I was sleeping on.

It took me some time to clear my head and make a plan. When I was able to string a few thoughts together, I started making phone calls in search of a ride. This was before cell phones were common. Danny gave me the address of the apartment. I was in Pacoima, which was not the best place to be a white boy wearing only a robe and slippers and carrying a half-ounce of blow. I was able to reach Mom, but she was not happy to hear from me. After I told her where I was and what I was wearing, she just hung up on me. When I called back with a second plea, my friend Al picked up the phone. He was at the house hanging out with Brett. I told Al about my unsafe situation, and he was able to convince Mom to pick me up. Luckily, I was not mugged or beaten up while I stood on the corner of a busy street in a bad part of town wearing only my boxer shorts, slippers, and a stupid robe waiting for my ride.

That was one of many drug adventures I had with Johnny. He was a great guy, and at the time, I considered him my brother. During a few of my homeless stints, he took me in and allowed me to sleep on a couch in the garage at his mom's house until his sister Holly complained about seeing me too often. It was so uncomfortable to have her walk by me in the mornings to do laundry when I was whacked out in the garage trying to sleep on the couch—fully clothed and curled up in a blanket, just trying to stay warm. Later, Johnny and I became dealing partners. That arrangement lasted until I made the mistake of passing out at another dealer's house while I had our pager on me.

I had been partying with another dealer named Carlos and his cousin, Angel. Angel and I got so high that we started drinking rubbing alcohol with Kool-Aid in it because we ran out of grain alcohol. We had plenty of blow, just not enough liquor. Finally, in order for me to chill, I swallowed a handful of Valium, and it knocked me out—for two full days. I came to forty-eight hours later in the middle of the floor in Carlos' empty apartment.

Johnny was so pissed at me for having the "business" pager on me that whole time that he fired me as his partner. Granted, in two days' time, we missed numerous orders, but he didn't fire me over lost business so much as because of my drug problem. I was really distressed by Johnny's decision, because he and I were really good friends, but it turned out to be a blessing in disguise. Less than a year after Johnny fired me, he was shot and killed while making a blow deal. If he and I had remained partners, I would have definitely been with him making that deal because of the large amount of blow that was being exchanged.

Johnny wasn't the only one to meet a gruesome end. The guy that I met that night in Pacoima, Danny, was found hanging in an apartment. Some guys took his quarter ounce of blow and then hung him. I heard the killers smoked his stash while he was swinging in front of them. My friend, Steve, the guy who'd followed me in his car while I rode my moped on the freeway, looking for the bags of blow Dad had thrown out the window, also met a gruesome end as the result of his cocaine addiction. He either ripped off the wrong guys or was wrongly accused of it. Either way, he and his family both suffered the consequences. Steve's body was chopped up into pieces and mailed piece by piece to his parents. I was privy to the details of so many horrific drug-related deaths. It is an absolute miracle that I did not meet with a similar end.

CHAPTER 20
AGE 19

While I was living at Mom's in Chatsworth, Brett was living in Salt Lake City with Dad. Brett called me one night because he knew some guys in Utah who wanted to score a quarter pound of blow. I told my mom I was going out to dinner with some friends and instead went off on yet another idiotic drug-dealing adventure. I hopped a plane to Utah to do the deal, which went off without a hitch. Afterwards, I decided to hang out and party a couple of days with Brett.

I hadn't seen my Dad for three years, so Brett and I decided to not let him know I was in town, especially since Mom thought I was still in LA. Nevertheless, Dad found out I was in town doing a drug deal. I am convinced that Brett's girlfriend was the one who let it slip. Once he found out, he called a meeting at his fiancée's home. With arrogance and fear, I met him.

During this talk with him, his fiancée, and her children, I was confronted about doing the drug deal. At first, I calmly denied everything, but once I realized my back was against the wall, I did what I usually did. I blew up. I started screaming that, yes, I was a fucking drug dealer, and there wasn't anything he could do about it. Once I'd opened the dam, there was no stopping the torrent. I let him have it—full force. I pulled out the stacks of cash I had on me and waved the drug money in front of his face. I even pulled out the gun I had in my jacket. I screamed, "This is me, your fucking drug-dealing son! Are you proud of me? The son you raised? Or better yet, the son you abandoned?" With that parting shot, I stormed out of the house. I always knew just what to say to cause the most damage, the worst pain. **Sadly, it was usually those I loved the most who I hurt the worst.**

Not long after returning to LA, I had the same kind of manic flare up in a similar situation with Mom and Sam. I had just sworn to Mom that I was not dealing when my pager went off in my pocket. Timing really is everything. It was as if a game show buzzer had sounded because I'd given the wrong answer. In those days, there was only one reason a nineteen-year-old would have a pager. When my pager went off, brazenly contradicting the promise I'd just made, I felt caught.

"You are lying to me," she accused.

That's when I detonated. "Yeah, I am a fucking drug dealer, just leave me alone." This contemptuous statement did not go over well at all. Sam called the police, and then we got into a full-on brawl. Mom jumped on my back and wrapped her arms around me, trying, fruitlessly, to restrain me. The fight continued, fists flying, until the cops arrived. She and Sam informed the police that I was dealing drugs. The authorities told them there wasn't anything they could do about it unless there was proof to substantiate their charge, which they could not provide. The cops gave me a long lecture about how drug dealing would only lead to trouble. **Of course, this boring speech went in one ear and out the other.**

My days of dealing drugs out of the townhouse basement were soon over—they kicked me out. From then on, I lived in one motel room after another. Sometimes I would have several motel rooms at different motels at the same time. I'd have one room filled with friends partying, another reserved just for me—for when I was too high to be around anyone else, and finally, a room just for my cocaine. I kept my scale and my entire stash of blow in that room, and I would use the room to weigh it out for sale.

Out of paranoia, I found the craziest places to hide blow while living in these motel rooms. I pinned it up in drapes, stashed it in holes I'd ripped in mattresses, or tucked it behind pictures mounted on the wall. Although I met many buyers myself, I often sent "runners" to meet people for me. Sometimes I had limos driving us to and from the different motels because we were all too high to drive. I felt like a big shot—the big idiot drug dealer! I might have been able to make a go of it as a "high rolling" dealer, but the gruesome ends that Steve, Danny, and Johnny met with when they were "high-rolling" kept me from risking the next level. And frankly, I was too much of an addict myself to keep a "high-rolling" operation together.

I actually did own a car during this time in my life—the 280 ZX from Miami had found its way back to me because my cousin Ed used it to drive himself cross-country from Miami to Los Angeles to live. However, for many months, I could not even find the car. I had forgotten where I parked it and simply lived without wheels until some friends of mine happened to see it parked on a random street. The crazy thing was that even after locating my car, I had no idea how it ended up there. All I could remember was waking up after a long run at my friend Tim's parents' house and not knowing where my car was.

Tim was a childhood friend from junior high. His nickname was "Sticks" because of how skinny he was from doing blow. He and I went on numerous drug runs. Stick's brother was nicknamed Magoo. I can't even remember his real name. Magoo was part of an Irish gang called "The Wilbur Boys," who always partied together and got into a lot of street fights. The main man of the gang was nicknamed Finny. We called him "Finny me-lad." It was nice to be connected with this gang because I knew I had backup if I ever needed it. I spent many days partying with that gang. After I stopped hanging out with them, I found out that some of them got busted for making counterfeit money and Finny was murdered.

During this time, I somehow talked Mom into allowing me to stay with her again, at least on a temporary basis. One night, Sticks and I took Mom's company car on one of our outings. Again, I couldn't remember where I'd parked the 280 ZX, so I borrowed her car with the understanding that I would absolutely have it back to her by the end of the night. She had an important business appointment the next day.

Sticks and I were partying with some girls who, as it turned out, were not into blow. We decided to ditch the girls and go score. I was drunk though and totaled the car when I lost control on a tight corner. I drove it over a curb and straight into a brick wall. Somehow Sticks and I were not badly hurt, just shook up a bit and unwilling to give up on the score; so I drove the car anyway, although the front tires were both flat, the hood was completely smashed up and blocked my view, and the steering wheel was tilted oddly from where my body had hit it. A few blocks down the road, I pulled into a grocery store parking lot, and we abandoned the car there. We hitched a ride and were able to score. We partied for the next three days straight. I never called Mom to tell her where her car was.

That was one of the most uncomfortable partying sessions I ever had and probably the worst thing I ever did to my mom. She paged me repeatedly over the next few days. I felt horrible each time, but I never called her back. I was too high. All I needed to do was just let her know where her car was so that she could get a tow truck or something, but I couldn't do it. I was so whacked out that I just ignored each page and tried to convince myself that I had never totaled her car.

The first day, I must have gotten fifty pages from her, the second day—twenty-five, the third—a dozen, and so on, until the pages began coming in only sporadically. Finally, about ten days later, Al called me to say that she had stopped by his place with a suitcase of my stuff. She left it there with him and told him to tell me to never come home again. After I heard this, I left her a message letting her know where her car was.

That was the last time I had any communication with Mom for close to a year. Once again, I was homeless and living in motel rooms and sleeping on friends' couches, in garages, or in cars. I saw her about a year later at a grocery store. I was buying baking soda to cook rock. We practically walked right into each other. Humbly, I said, "Hello." She looked into my eyes and asked, "Do I know you?" then walked away. Ordinarily, **I was emotionally numb from the constant drug use,** but this penetrated the numbness. It was one of the saddest moments of my life.

CHAPTER 21
AGE 20

After some time on the streets and in motels, I found myself living with Adam Rich. Adam was a child star from the hit TV series "Eight is Enough." Before my drug use became rampant, Adam had been my best friend. He had started avoiding me when I went totally off the deep end and began dealing and running the streets. He caught me one night going to Johnny's house to get a gun to kill this guy, Ted. Ted had ripped me off, stealing some of my money and some of my blow. Adam looked at me as I was getting the gun and, with great compassion, asked, "Now you're killing people, too?" He sounded deeply disappointed. "Wow, I never thought of you that way." It hit me. I was stunned. I had never thought of myself that way either. Even though I had acted tough many times to protect myself on the street, I had never killed anyone, and I decided that I didn't want to start.

Adam took me in with the single requirement—no dealing. I made and kept that promise, for a time. I wish that meant my life turned around, but it did not. Instead, it turned Adam's life around. He got as ugly for drugs as I was. Adam and I lived together in a rented condo at Van Patten Place. The building was owned by Dick Van Patten, who'd played Adam's father on *Eight is Enough*. Adam and I partied hard there. We would be up for days using and then swearing, time and time again, **"This is it! We are done basing! We are done!"** We would promise each other over and over, but to no avail. We would break all the paraphernalia, pipes, torches, blades, and vials, only to repair or replace them after a few days' rest and after we got some food in our stomachs. As soon as we felt a little better, we'd start all over again. **It was a vicious cycle.**

* * *

At some point during all this, we hooked up with my old Cupertino High School friend, Dieter. For the next few months, Dieter, Adam, and I hung out, smoked rock, and ate a lot of acid. This was my second round of acid days. Our motto was, "Take two, they're small." The three of us dropped a couple of hits of acid a day for so many days in a row that eventually we had to take over ten hits at a time just to get off a little. We had sheets of acid and ounces of blow with us at all times. We routinely drove from LA to San Diego to hook up with our friend Al, who was attending San Diego State at the time. We hit all the fraternity parties whacked out on blow and acid.

On any given road trip, we pulled stupid stunts, many of which could have landed us in serious trouble. Our outrageous behavior never drew the wrong kind of attention though, and astonishingly, we never got busted. Well, at least Adam and I never got busted. Dieter wasn't as lucky. Dieter and I were trying to get him on a plane to deliver six ounces of blow and a few sheets of acid to some buyers in the Bay area. During the drive to the airport on the 405 freeway, we were cooking and smoking rock in the car, and we were too high to make it on time to his flight. We arrived at the Los Angeles airport too late, then turned around and tried to catch the next flight out of the Burbank airport. And so on—back and forth. We finally got him on a plane to San Francisco, where, days later, at a Dead show, the police busted him for selling all the blow and acid to an undercover cop.

Then there were the times that we carried massive amounts of drugs back and forth across the Mexican border. I carried ounces of blow with me into Tijuana while I was tripping on acid, openly handing out bindles of cocaine to friends and strangers at El Torito's Restaurant in Mexico, without making any effort to conceal what I was doing. I would often audaciously take out a baggy of blow, crush rocks between my fingers and snort them while sitting at the same bar as the Federales, the Mexican federal police. I thought I was the big shot dealer, and Al and his girlfriend confirmed it for me when they told me they'd overheard people in that Mexican bar refer to me as "the coke dealer from LA."

Those days with Adam were some of the ugliest and most despondent for me, but that's not to say we didn't have some fun times, too. **That is the problem with being an addict and alcoholic. Thousands of bad experiences that destroy our lives are forgotten while we chase the memories of the few good experiences we've had.**

Ultimately, Adam's money began to get tight, so I talked him into letting me break my promise about not dealing. I went back to dealing and was then able to keep the blow flowing for a while longer. Eventually, I did another deal with the guys from Utah. During this deal, I met a girl named Tammy who eventually became my girlfriend. Tammy partied a little but was definitely not an addict. She was a good, wholesome girl who, unfortunately, got entangled in my chaotic drug world.

Months later, Tammy talked me into moving to Utah to live with her in a small town called St. George. I thought it might be a good idea since my goal was to mellow out and try to get my life together. I was almost twenty and did not have anything going for me. I was living on Adam's couch and only selling enough drugs to keep our own stash full.

I called Mom before I left for Utah, both to let her know what I was doing and to ask her for help in starting a new life. I had not spoken with her in over a year and was so thankful that she did not hang up the phone on me. I shared with her that I believed the only way that I could get my life together was to move out of Los Angeles and try to go back to school. After a series of phone calls and, yet again, many promises, Mom agreed to give me the financial assistance I needed to attend a college with Tammy in St George, Utah.

Once I arrived there, I thought St. George was a joke. It was a very small town with very small town thinking. I hated it there and everyone knew it. I quickly became known as the drug dealer from LA, which was helpful in some relationships and damaging in others. I still made deals with the group from Salt Lake City. I didn't last more than six months in St. George. I convinced Tammy to move back to California with me. I didn't want to go back to Los Angeles, so we ended up in San Luis Obispo. She attended Cuesta College, and I just told Mom that I did. That lie was very damaging to our relationship.

My first semester at Cuesta, I failed everything. After the first few classes, I forgot which ones I was signed up for and where they were, so I just stopped going. The detailed lies I told my mom when she called were ridiculous. I made up stories about each class' content and then lied about my grades when the semester ended. It was nuts. I had learned something though. The second semester, I was smart enough to withdraw from each of my classes before the deadline.

My relationship with Tammy lasted only a short time in San Luis Obispo. When my drug use got the best of me, she couldn't take it anymore. I did not blame her. I stayed out just about every night, leaving her home alone, or, if I was home, we weren't alone. People came by at all hours of the night. She didn't like that I was dealing at the house. She got tired of all of the drug madness, even though I was pulling my life together better than at any other time. At least, I was "enrolled" in college—even if I wasn't attending.

CHAPTER 22

AGE 20

Like any good addict, I found all the other people who liked to use drugs in San Luis Obispo. But I was surprised to find that the other users thought I was a little out of control. In fact, I found out years later when I was sober that, in San Luis Obispo, I had once again earned my old nickname—the Devil. I taught many people how to freebase and supplied many more with massive amounts of blow. I made numerous drug runs down to LA, increasing the supply in and around San Luis Obispo.

There was a time during all of this that **I thought I had a handle on my drug use** and attempted to curb my sales. I went for a few weeks at a time not partying quite as hard and could, thereby, rationalize that I didn't need to quit because I could control it. I was not freebasing every night. I had not eaten acid or mushrooms in months, and I had not stuck a needle in my arm in years. I felt like I was starting to use like a "normal" person again. **That is the insanity of every addict. He believes he can drink and use like a "normal" person.**

Smoking pot, of course, did not count, because as far as I was concerned, it was not really a drug. In my mind, I could smoke pot daily and not be affected by it and I did. In fact, other than my visit to rehab and the period of time after those visits, there were not more than fifteen days in total, since I'd began using drugs, that I had not smoked pot. Smoking pot was normal for me, and I never imagined my life wouldn't include it. My goal was to rein in my use of *real* drugs, which continued to be a challenge.

While attempting to attend my second semester of college, I met a guy named Lowell who knew these guys in Palos Verdes who wanted to pick up a kilo of blow. I had been the middleman on the sale of several kilos before, and this was the same setup. I would meet and buy from two old friends of mine from high school, Darren and Randy, who had driven up to San Luis Obispo to drop off kilos for me to sell. This time, however, I was driving to them in Los Angeles.

I met Kevin, one of the guys from Palos Verdes, who gave me the money and loaned me his car for the pickup. Then, I drove to a fast food restaurant in the San Fernando Valley where I met Darren and made the exchange. I put the pack (kilo) under the car seat and drove back to deliver the blow and return the car. I showed Kevin where the pack was under the seat and asked, more likely begged, him to break the window and chip me off some to take with me. (The "window" is a square inch of cellophane in the middle of the cast surrounding the blow. It can be broken to test the blow inside.) The pack's window was intact. Kevin said he didn't want to break the window because he was turning it over the next day, and he wanted the pack to be clean. I persisted with my request that he open it and bust me out a little blow for the drive home, but he refused.

The next day, the shit hit the fan. Kevin called to say that the blow was fake! I didn't believe it at first. I thought he was bullshitting, because I'd known the guys I got the blow from for years. It just didn't seem possible that my old friends, guys who'd been down this same road with me so many times, would knowingly scam me. I could hear that this was a big problem for Kevin and the other guys on his end of the deal. They were freaking out. I told them to chill and that I would get it all sorted out.

I called Darren and Randy over and over. No answer. I called dozens of mutual friends and learned that my worst suspicions were true. Darren and Randy had been on a rampage, ripping people off by selling bunk packs and purchasing good ones with counterfeit money. I was blown away, pissed off, and now freaking out with fear! This was a problem—a serious one! How the hell was I going to make this good and get myself out of this mess? I was not in a financial position to pay them back, nor did I know of anyone who would be willing to step up and pay them to save my ass. One of Kevin's guys had already threatened me; he told me that if I did not get Kevin his money, he would kidnap me and sell my ass on West Hollywood Boulevard until he was reimbursed.

There wasn't any alternative. I had to go back down to LA and meet Kevin and his posse. Afterward, I'd take them over to Darren and Randy's to get this all sorted out. I had already been told that these guys would want to know where each of Darren's and Randy's parents lived as well. They knew I'd known them for many years. It was logical to assume I'd know where their families lived. I drove back down to LA with Lowell, who'd introduced me to these guys in the first place. I had no idea what was in store for me. My assumption was that, because I was "on their team," when I'd explained to them that I hadn't ripped them off, they'd believe me. Their response was a big surprise for me.

Instead, the second I got out of the car, I was grabbed by two huge, very angry guys who threw me against the car and punched me. They loudly demanded, "Where is our fucking money?" Then one of them grabbed my head, squeezed it between his hands, leaned in and started biting my nose so hard I thought for sure he was going to bite it off. As soon as he stopped biting, I started talking—very fast. I was trying to get the message across that I had not ripped them off. I was there to help! They weren't hearing me. "Shut the fuck up! You better get our fucking money!" It was the only response I got.

I gave them directions to Randy's house, and the guy who'd

been biting my nose told me I was going to get a bullet up my ass that night. He wanted to know how I felt about making the eleven o'clock news, along with my parents. They even announced Mom's address, so that I would know they knew where she and Sam lived. The fact that they knew where my family lived made me sick inside. It was then that I realized the true gravity of the situation.

Leaving Lowell behind, the four of us—Kevin, his two goons, and I—arrived at Randy's house and approached the front porch. The two thugs each pulled out a sawed-off shotgun, and Kevin pulled out a pistol. They positioned themselves on either side of the front door. I was told to knock on the door, and as I did, I pictured Randy opening the door, guns blazing and me stupidly standing in the middle of this shoot out. I wondered whether Randy being there would get me off the hook or if his presence would get me shot for sure.

Randy was not home, which infuriated my nose-biting friend. I heard all about it on the way back to the car, where I was pistol whipped and again thrown into the backseat. At this point, I saw the coffin lid closing on me. Randy was not home, these guys were pissed, and I had nothing to give them. When we got back to the car, they insisted I take them to Randy's parents' house. We were escorted there by another friend of mine who knew where they lived. Randy's little sister was in the front yard, and I had this terrible feeling they were going to do something to her. Fortunately, they did not. We just drove by. But if they had to, they all agreed, they would come back for her later.

This was when the full magnitude of how despicable the drug business is hit me. I flashed on the scene in the movie *Scarface,* where the guy was chain-sawed in the shower. I had never actually acknowledged the fact that people got killed over drugs. **People got killed over what I dealt. It didn't just happen in the movies, it happened all the time.** I knew that.

It had happened to guys I'd known, friends, and partners—but deep down; I did not ever think it would happen the way it was happening that night. It really woke me up. **Suddenly I was disgusted with myself. I realized that, like it or not, I was a real part of this truly horrific, deplorable, and destructive drug world.**

In the middle of all this madness, God came rushing into my consciousness. I started praying for God to get me out of this one, and if he did, I promised I was going to get sober again. It's interesting that every time the shit hit the fan, I went begging and pleading to God, bartering for my life. I made so many deals with God during my using days, but I never held up my end of the bargain. Not once. And yet, **God came through for me every time.**

As these internal prayers to God were taking place, we drove back to see if Randy was home yet. These guys were telling me that if he wasn't there, I had better think of a way to get their money or I was going to get a bullet in my ass. This is when I made my final appeal to Kevin, who was driving the car. I pleaded my innocence, denied any involvement, and continued my testimony of self-defense over the ranting of the nose-biter and his pal.

I was talking fast and making sense in spite of getting smacked upside the head after every other sentence by the nose-biter. There was screaming in the car from everyone, except for Kevin, who remained silent. I loudly reminded him that I had wanted him to break the window and that I was there now to straighten this out. The other guys in the car kept screaming at me to "Shut the fuck up!" There was so much commotion and hollering in the car that I had to yell, "Kevin, if I was going to sting you, why the fuck would I have asked you to break the window, and why the fuck would I be here now?" I kept repeating my case until Kevin suddenly pulled the car over. He opened his door and got out of the car.

"Get the fuck out of here," he said, letting me out of the back.

"Today is your lucky day." I almost started crying, and at the same time, I could not get out of the car fast enough.

My nose fetish buddy was yelling at Kevin, "What the fuck are you talking about? Fuck this punk! Fuck him! I am going to put a cap in his head!"

"Let's just go get Randy," I heard Kevin say, but I was already out of the car and running for my life. I have forgotten now how far I ran or for how long. Everything was a total blur. I was not sure where I was running to at first, but then I found myself running back to the place where Lowell had dropped me off. His car was still parked in the same place, and as I approached, I saw him with his head down. When I abruptly opened the passenger side door to jump in, he looked up, startled, with tears running down his face. When he saw me, I could tell he thought he was seeing a ghost.

"Get the fuck out of here!" I advised.

He asked, "Oh my God! What the fuck happened?"

"Just drive. Please just drive us out of here as fast as possible!" I replied. Lowell obliged. As we drove out of the area, he expressed his relief. He said he had been sure I was dead. He knew how dangerous those guys were. The nose-biter had killed some people Lowell knew. He also explained that he was still parked there because he didn't know whether they expected him to stay or not.

While Lowell talked, I reached into the glove box and pulled out some papers and weed. I needed to roll a doobie. As my fingers worked, my head was full of shame. Not thirty minutes earlier, I had pleaded with God. I promised that I would get sober if He got me out of that situation. He kept his side of the bargain. I was still alive. I was in Lowell's car. And what was I doing? I was preparing to get high.

I started justifying myself to God. "You have to understand," I told Him, "I am a partier. It's in my blood. This is what I do.

I cannot help it, and I cannot change." Like any good addict, I thought I could renegotiate the terms. I explained to God that I was grateful and I owed Him. In exchange for his understanding, I assured Him I would not sell blow any more. That was as close as I could come to honoring the deal I made with God as I begged for my life in Kevin's car.

CHAPTER 23

AGE 20 – 22

It got much worse before my using days finally came to an end. Looking back on it, I thank God that it got worse. If it hadn't, I most likely would have kept trying to control my using. I would have certainly been caught up in more and more craziness. After escaping the bad deal incident and returning to San Luis Obispo, I was able to barely finish a semester of college. I continued drinking and smoking pot daily. And when school let out, I headed back to LA to stay with Mom and Sam for the summer.

Once there, I hooked up with my old friends and the partying continued. I had sworn off dealing and even attempted to swear off blow as a result of the bunk blow fiasco. I did manage to refrain from dealing, but was unable to stay away from the blow. I had promised my mom, my girlfriends, and many good friends who were looking after me, and even God that I would stop. Over and over again, I had promised, but I failed to keep my promise every time.

The disease of alcoholism and addiction is absolutely cunning and baffling! Despite the most horrific consequences, once addicted, nothing gets in the way of acquiring drugs and using. Every time I had sworn off drugs, it had been with complete conviction, but the disease blots out the consequences of using and the reasons not to quit.

I made it very clear to everyone back in LA that I was not going to make any deals to fill our stash. For the most part, everyone understood. Unfortunately, however, we were all running out of money. Adam still had a little money left from his acting career, and we continued to party mostly on his dime those last few months, but something was different—the blow stopped getting me high. We smoked rock for days, and then, after a long run, we would start all over again. It was hell. My first hit off the pipe was like the last one from a long binge. Those of you who have been on long blow binges know that by the end of the binge, you are no longer getting high; you are just prolonging the comedown. I couldn't get that initial rush anymore, even though I tried over and over to attain it.

Another thing started happening to me physically. **My body was going numb.** I would sit on the couch and not move because I was sweating and experiencing tingling sensations. I wouldn't be able to feel parts of my body. I would be afraid to get up in case I'd urinated on myself or worse—had a bowel movement without knowing it. I would constantly look down at my crotch to see if there was any discoloration. Any time I got up, I went straight to the restroom to check myself. I never actually soiled myself, but the constant suspicion that I might have freaked me out. It was extremely uncomfortable and disconcerting, and yet it still did not deter my drug use.

Everything came crashing down around me in a few weeks' time. **My tolerance disappeared. My body could no longer handle what I continued to put into it, and it was shutting down.** I feared my mind was going. My memory certainly was. **I couldn't stop partying, but I couldn't keep partying either—and I couldn't moderate.** During this time, we happened to have a large supply of generic Quaaludes called Gorilla Biscuits, and I was eating them like candy and often having total blackouts. When I came to, everyone else would have to tell me what I had been doing. I came out of a blackout on one occasion with a cut and bruise over my eye. Apparently, I had run into a tree. Later that same night, I spent some time rolled up in a rug for my own protection. My brother and his friends improvised a straightjacket for me to prevent me from hurting myself further. I don't remember any of it.

I have intermittent memories of another night at Adam's. Adam, Brett, Al, Sticks, and I were all there partying. I was completely wasted on the biscuits, Valium, alcohol, and blow and I had been up for a day or so already, which compounded the effects of everything. I was really out of it, bordering on delirium. I was higher on the biscuits and Valium than anything else, and I kept nodding out.

I remember thinking, "Shit, I'm going to nod out and die." I could barely keep it together. I was seeing things and hearing things. That was when I mumbled, "Rick, is that you? Rick, what did you say?" Everyone around me started laughing and saying, "Oh my God, Rob is so fucked up." I stared blankly with glossy eyes at the place where I had just seen Rick, wondering stupidly what he'd just said and where he'd gone. How had he disappeared so quickly? Then, my friends told me that Rick had not been with us for days, which kind of freaked me out because I'd just been having a conversation with him. I remained silent and continued to search the room. I didn't see Rick, but a pile of blow on the table caught my attention. I decided to stick my face into it and snort while inhaling at the same time. I had blow all over my face and in my mouth. This was not a popular decision with the rest of the group, so they carried me to Adam's room to lie down.

I lay there on Adam's bed, more stoned than I had ever been. I couldn't say anything, so I just listened to the reverberations of the voices and noises around me. I remember Al saying, "Oh my God, he is so fucked up!" His words echoed around me as if I were in a bell. I remember Sticks laughing. I heard the concern in my brother's voice when he told everyone to shut the fuck up, that this was serious, and that they ought to take me to the hospital to have my stomach pumped. Then Adam said, "Let me take his pulse." A moment passed and he said, "No, he is going to be okay."

I remember thinking, "Now, that's my boy, a true hero and partner in knowing a good high. Do not move me! This is utopia. I am about to go out." Like the lyrics by Pink Floyd, I had become "comfortably numb." **I didn't care if I died that night. I was in a drug addict's heaven—completely stoned and numb. I couldn't move or talk.** I just laid there and listened.

A day or two later, I got it together, ate some food, and slept it off. As always, I broke my promise with God and started dealing now and then to fill our stash. I was able to do a deal and pick up a quarter ounce of blow. I called Adam to tell him so we could go to his place and party. He told me I was not going to believe what he had. When he told me, I commanded, "Do not go *anywhere*, I'll be right there to pick you up!" Adam had a full rig of morphine. I drove like a maniac to Adam's parents' house, sweating and craving it the entire drive. When I got there, I jumped out of my car, raced up to the door, and knocked enthusiastically. I was hardly able to contain myself. As soon as Adam opened the door, I barked, "Where is it?"

"Shut up! Be quiet!" He motioned for me to calm down, and then pulled the rig out of his shirt pocket. I snatched it out of his hands and dropped my pants right there in the doorway of his parents' home. Adam hissed at me to stop, trying not to be loud. I did not and could not. I stabbed my ass with the needle, right there in the entryway, and shot myself with more than half the rig.

I stumbled away from the house to the curb to lie down. Then I listened to Adam lecture me about being an idiot. I was sweating, rushing, and getting really high, or "low," as we called it, on the downs. Later that night, Adam and I went to his place to smoke the blow I had copped. In the middle of the night, we called two hookers to come over. That was a first for me. The last thing I recall about that night was screaming like a maniac at one of the hookers, who was sitting fully dressed on the couch, smoking a cigarette, and watching me. I wanted her to have sex with me, but I didn't want to use a condom.

As I stood naked in the middle of the room, I realized that I was being a complete idiot. I was embarrassed and acutely aware of what I needed to do. I stomped over to Adam's room, pounded on his door to roust him and the other prostitute. "These chicks need to get the hell out," I yelled.

The next day, when I thought about what had happened, I realized that things were getting really out of hand. I had broken the promise I'd made to myself to never use a needle again. I also felt bad about breaking my promise to God regarding dealing. I was completely embarrassed about being with the hookers. **I was physically falling apart at the age of twenty-two, and worse, I really wasn't getting high anymore.** Even smoking that entire quarter ounce hadn't gotten me that high. I knew it was all ending, and so, one more time, I pledged to quit. I couldn't take all of this insanity anymore. **It never occurred to me that I would not be able to stop on my own.**

CHAPTER 24
AGE 22

It was a Tuesday. I know because I remember thinking there was a really cool twelve-step meeting called Two-Plus-Two that I used to go to on Tuesdays, and it occurred to me that I could go that day. The idea, however, of attending an AA meeting made me incredibly nervous. My mind raced. Was I *really* going to try to get sober again? Could I do it? Was I done? Would I be able to do the work necessary to stay sober? Was I going to have to go back to a lockdown rehab again? **The excitement at the possibility of a new life, the anxiety of having to start all over with sobriety, the fear of doing something different, and the depression from thinking that I might not be able to get high again all ran through me as I considered going to that meeting.**

An hour or so before the time that I should've left for the meeting, I found a joint that I still had in a drawer. I smoked it and had a few swigs of tequila from Mom and Sam's bar. I felt a little calmer after that, so I decided to attend the meeting—high. I got there late. I nervously walked up to the meeting and, as I did, I saw someone sitting alone on a bench outside the meeting smoking a cigarette. As I got closer, I recognized my friend Richard. I couldn't believe it. Richard was the very last person I'd seen before I left for Miami. And there he was, like he was waiting for me to get sober again. How freaky was that? He looked up and recognized me too. His first words were, "Oh my fucking God—I thought you were dead!"

Richard and I shared stories and briefly brought each other up to date. He was very kind and encouraged me to get sober. He was glad that I had come to the meeting. So was I. The two of us went in and listened to what was left of the meeting. Afterwards, we exchanged phone numbers and made arrangements to meet the following evening for another meeting. At that very moment, I was convinced that I wanted sobriety and was ready to commit to it and The Program and I told Richard as much. I was done! I could not keep using drugs anymore. I wanted nothing more than to stay sober and change my life. I could tell Richard was really excited that I wanted sobriety and that he was happy to have me back again—alive.

Five minutes after the meeting ended, I became very uncomfortable and confused. What was I going to do now? I wasn't sure what to do or where to go. I was fearful that I was not going to be able to fall asleep and would, therefore, have to get high. Richard hadn't been gone five minutes, and I was already wavering. Standing there with him, I was convinced I wouldn't get high anymore, but now, alone, I wondered how I could avoid it. Then it hit me. I had already taken something that day, so the next day was going to be day one, no matter what I did that night. I figured that since I hadn't had a day of sobriety yet, I might as well get high that night and start day one tomorrow. That made sense and comforted me.

So I called my friend, Mark. Mark was a blow and bud dealer, and he had taken me in a number of times when I was on the streets. I think he felt a little indebted to me because I had taught him how to deal and introduced him to a few people. He was a much better dealer than I was, though, because he was not an addict. He partied, but not like an addict. I intended to call Mark and see if he had any buds to smoke. I didn't want to do any blow, just bid my using life a mellow farewell by smoking a little herb. Then I could wake up in the morning and stay sober for the rest of my life. That was all. That way, too, I could get a good night's sleep in order to start on my journey of recovery. I cleverly disguised my desire to get high with good intentions, as I had many times before. I remember all the different rationalizations I gave myself in my earlier attempts at sobriety to justify getting high one more time. **It's amazing how ingenious we addicts can be when it comes to postponing the end, finding any reason to justify to others or ourselves why we need to party** *one more time.*

My revised conviction while driving to Mark's was that no matter what, I would not ask if he had any blow. I swore it to myself over and over on the way there. *I am just going to smoke pot and bail. Go home, get to sleep, and get sober.* This became my mantra driving there. I walked into Mark's place with a strong resolve to steer clear of blow, only to find him sitting there with a kilo of coke cracked open on the table in front of him. As soon as I was through the door, he said, "Hey, you're good at this. Tell me what this is washed with." Here is the insane part. Without the slightest hesitation, I walked over and took a snort and told him it was washed with kerosene. I was so upset with myself, but at the same time, I had gotten that rush, and I knew the party was on.

At that moment, I was convinced of my absolute powerlessness over drugs. On the way over there, I'd promised myself, repeatedly, that I was not going to do any blow. I swore to myself with absolute conviction that I wouldn't. I meant it to the core of my being. In fact, it was perhaps the most genuine promise that I ever made to myself during my loaded days—and it lasted until the second I saw the blow. **That experience helped me realize the power drugs had over me.** I'd known it before, but not to the same extent. This was a new, truer, and deeper realization. If

I'd had any doubt before, it was now gone.

Mark and I lined it up for a few hours until I convinced him to let me cook some up to smoke. He and I smoked out until the next day. Then, in normal Mark fashion, he was done and told me he was going to go to sleep—and he did. I never understood that guy. He went to his room and locked the door. I never understood how Mark and other "normal" users were able to stop themselves like that. It always made me think the same way about them, "They're fucking weirdos!"

I lay there on Mark's couch, feeling totally whacked out and paranoid. All kinds of thoughts ran through my head about AA and getting sober. The first step of The Program's twelve kept running through my mind. It says, "We came to believe that we were powerless over alcohol and that our lives had become unmanageable." Lying there half dead, in a stone-cold sweat, speechless, and unable to move a muscle, this step, uninvited and unwanted, began to haunt me.

There was a part of me that thought, "Oh fuck, how did I get myself back into that fucking AA program shit?" Disgusted with myself, I fumed, "Great, now I am going to have Richard calling me and trying to get me sober. All those fucking cultish, brainwashing AAs are going to be all up in my shit. How am I going to get out of this one?" As the hours rolled by, the mental rollercoaster began. I started substituting the thought of wanting to get out of meeting Richard with the thought that perhaps I wanted to meet him. Maybe I wanted to get sober after all.

I thought about all my partying years. All the mistakes, fuck-ups, and problems that had ever occurred in my life were due to my drug use. Drugs were also now taking a physical toll on my body. I thought about the dreams of being a professional athlete I had thrown away, all the criminal acts I had committed, and all the people I had ripped off—all just to get high. And the worst part was that the drugs were not getting me as high as they once had. The problems that had developed because of my use far outweighed the pleasure the highs now delivered. **I was chasing a high that wasn't even that good anymore. My life was a total wreck, a shame, and an embarrassment.** I was a loser, just as Dad had prophesized.

As I was lying there, plagued by thoughts and trying to sleep, the phone kept ringing. Neither Mark nor I ever answered it. Once Mark was out, there was no waking him. The answering machine picked up each time, and I could hear my girlfriend's voice getting increasingly frustrated as she continued to leave messages.

The guilt I felt about breaking my commitments, compounded with the guilt I felt about breaking my promise to Richard and myself, weighed heavily on me. I thought about my complete mess of a life, all of the factors that had led up to my going to that meeting, and the eerie coincidence of seeing Richard there. Suddenly, I thought, "If I can get off this couch and out of Mark's place and lock the door behind me, maybe I can make it through the day without using." I didn't have any drugs in any pockets, drawers, under any car seats, or at friends' houses. I was totally out of everything. I was dry. And if I could get out of there, drive home, and chill until that evening, I might be able to at least stay sober for the day.

As I got off the couch, I was unsure of what I was doing. I was torn between knocking on Mark's door to request a bong load to calm down and just getting out of his place and following my plan. I stood in his living room for a few minutes trying to decide, until I ultimately realized that Mark would not get up anyway. I was forced to stick to my plan. I got to his front door, opened it, made sure it was locked behind me and slowly shut the door. The second it was shut, I almost started crying. I wanted to open it again. I was so scared. I did not want to get sober. I did not want to do the work of sobriety. I did not want to have to endure those cravings to get high that would certainly be in my future if I chose sobriety. I did not want to listen to all those fucking sober-preaching therapeutic fuckheads tell me how to run my life. **I was scared, angry, and confused.**

I managed to drive to Mom's house and lay down to sleep. I woke up at around five that evening, just in time to receive Richard's call to meet him for a meeting. I did not tell him about the night I'd had at Mark's. Somehow, I was able to leave the house to go meet Richard without hitting Mom's bar for liquor.

When I got to the meeting, I didn't say much to anyone other than Richard. He and I chatted more about the years apart. At the beginning of the meeting, the secretary asked if there were any newcomers in their first thirty days of sobriety who would care to introduce themselves. Of course I qualified, but I didn't raise my hand. I did not want a bunch of sober dorks coming up to me and welcoming me and giving me their phone numbers.

The whole meeting I listened and related to the story of the speaker and those who shared afterwards. I knew I was doomed if I continued using. I knew my life had zero possibilities if I did not stop living this way. And **I knew that if I did not stop, I would likely end up dead or in prison.** I was not afraid of dying, but I was absolutely terrified of prison. **I knew I needed to get sober. I just wasn't sure I could stay sober.** Towards the end of the meeting, I got up to use the restroom. As I walked back in through the door of the meeting, I heard the secretary ask, "Is there anyone here in their first day of sobriety?" Completely of its own volition, my hand went up. I could not believe it. It seemed like I didn't have any control of it. It just went up. As soon as it did, everyone in the room turned around and looked at me. The room, filled with all those sober dorks, went into immediate applause. At that very second, I had an overwhelming feeling of being welcomed, loved, of belonging, and of being at home. **I knew, right then and there, that my life had just changed.**

Part II

CHAPTER 1
AGE 22

My first meeting ended and Richard had to leave to meet a friend. After he left, I felt completely lost and unsure of myself. I didn't know what to do next. How was I going to get to sleep without putting something in my system? I had not slept without being intoxicated, drugged, or drinking bottles of Nyquil in years. These were the same fears I had experienced the previous night—and that had led me to Mark's. However, this time I did not have the same excuse to go and get high. If I was able to make it through the night, I would achieve one day of sobriety.

After the meeting, a few people who were going out for coffee were thoughtful enough to invite me. I jumped at the invitation, although I was not about to put any coffee into my system. The last thing I wanted was additional trouble getting to sleep that night. I went anyway, because I did not want to be alone.

When the meeting at the coffeehouse after the AA meeting was over, a girl named Patti invited me to come to her apartment to watch TV. I revealed to her that I was really uncomfortable and afraid that I would not be able to get to sleep that night. I hung out with her for a few hours and we talked about our past drug abuse. Patti shared with me how she was able to stay sober in The Program, despite her being around my age.

My youth had presented an added challenge to me the first time I had attempted sobriety back when I'd been a resident at Coldwater Canyon Hospital. I had just turned seventeen when I'd completed rehab at the hospital, and for the next six years, I hadn't been able to string together any consecutive time of abstinence. When I'd left rehab and started with AA, there hadn't been many young people involved. Years away from AA had brought big changes, and I was shocked at how many more young people were now in AA and at how long many of them had been able to maintain sobriety. Today it is much more common to see people who've never taken a legal-age drink come into the rooms. **Now there are thousands, if not millions, of sober young people in The Fellowship.** Patti told me that she knew dozens of sober people in their late teens and early twenties. It was comforting to know that I would not be the only sober person my age.

Later that night, after leaving Patti's, I drove up and down Pacific Coast Highway listening to music. I smoked half a pack of cigarettes. I was so afraid to go home and try to sleep. Finally, too tired to drive, I went home and, after lots of tossing and turning, fell asleep. When I woke up, I realized that I had almost accomplished one full day of sobriety. I partied until past midnight at Mark's house, so I still had several hours left before achieving my first twenty-four hours of abstinence. Nevertheless, I was excited. I felt very proud of myself. I had endured at least one night without being intoxicated or drugged to sleep, and I got up without taking anything. It was a huge accomplishment for me. **I started to have faith and confidence that I might be able to stay sober—at least for a day.**

I made a phone call on my first day to my old sponsor, Stuart. (A sponsor in a twelve-step program is a confidant or mentor who has already taken The Steps and is willing to take others through them in the same way. Members who are willing to sponsor others can be found at just about any meeting.) Stuart had worked at Coldwater Canyon Hospital during my stint there. He was supportive during my earlier attempt at sobriety, and I was always able to relate to him. He was about twenty years older, but we had forged a connection based on our common history of drug use and our goal to stay sober. Stuart was an ex-junkie who, coincidentally, knew my Aunt Dawn when she lived in Hollywood.

I disclosed to Stuart my apprehension about going into a lockdown rehab unit like Coldwater Canyon or any sober living house. I didn't want to do either, but I was convinced that I'd have to do one or the other to have any chance of staying sober. **I didn't think I could do this sober thing without being locked up.** I didn't have the slightest idea how to do it on my own or if it was possible.

Stuart asked me if I'd been able to stay sober yesterday. I told him, "Yes, sort of," and explained that it hadn't yet been a full twenty-four hours. He then suggested I stay sober for the rest of that day, get to a meeting that evening, and then go to sleep without taking anything. He told me to call him the next morning at ten unless I needed to talk to him sooner. It was a struggle for me to get up that early. I was used to sleeping all day and partying at night, but I wanted to get up as early as possible so that I would be extra tired at night and would fall asleep quicker. I feared being up until all hours of the night—alone. I knew that would have been a recipe for disaster.

My first full twenty-four hours of sobriety sucked! The whole day I kept asking myself, **"Do I really need this? What are my other options?"** I kept thinking of Monty Hall's game show from years ago called "Let's Make A Deal." In the show, the contestants are given three different possible prize options to choose from, each concealed by a curtain. In my case, however, there were only two curtains to choose between, and I didn't like what was behind either one of them. The way I saw it at the time, I could either continue using drugs and being miserable or I could live this AA bullshit sober life. I wanted another choice. I wanted curtain number three, but there was no curtain number three available to me.

I called Stuart on schedule and he asked me right off, "Well, were you able to make it for a full day without using?"

"Yeah, I was," I replied honestly. He wanted to know how I felt. I told him I felt great about trying to get sober but like shit physically, mentally, and emotionally.

Then he asked me if anyone had needed to lock me up so that I could attain this sobriety, which, of course, no one had. "Well then, for the time being, you do not have to be locked up," Stuart said matter-of-factly. "You were able to make it one day, and **that is all we have to do—stay sober one day at a time.**"

CHAPTER 2
AGE 22

I met Richard later that night for a meeting, and every night thereafter for over a week. I was getting to know more and more people my own age in The Fellowship. The best part was that I was staying sober. I was ecstatic and shocked! I felt like I was high the first few days that I wasn't using. I was so accustomed to being under the influence of something that using felt normal to me. **Being clean was strange. I felt weird. For me, sobriety was an altered state.** I was thinking clearly for the first time in years. I was aware of familiar surroundings and environments as if they were places I was experiencing for the first time.

Back when I was using, a bunch of friends once commented on the flurry of pages I was getting from customers. My friends said it must be for the big game.

"What big game?" I asked, and they laughed.

"You're kidding, right?" someone asked. Confused, I waited for them to explain, because I honestly had no idea what they were talking about. "The Super Bowl is tomorrow!" they exclaimed.

I was oblivious. After they told me that, it made me feel sad for a moment because I remembered how much I enjoyed watching the World Series and the Super Bowl as a kid. Everyone else quickly realized how out of touch I was, so they began testing me. "Hey, Sketch, what day of the week is it?" asked one. "Sketch, what *month* is it?" shouted another. Embarrassingly, I did not know. All that I knew was that it was kind of cold outside. I was completely lost.

Sober, my senses returned. I noticed fragrances in the air for the first time since I was a kid. I was aware of the temperature outside and the time of day—things normal people took for granted, but that I hadn't paid attention to in ages. Sometimes I noticed the smell of freebase, especially in some soaps and hair shampoos and it frightened me. I loved that smell so much. When that happened, I had to immediately get a new smell into my nose. Otherwise, I would begin to obsess on the memory of base. I was certain that obsession would lead me to act on it.

The days turned into weeks that became two months. Before I knew it, I had been sober for over sixty days! How the hell did that happen? It was amazing! During those first months of sobriety, I dealt with my fear of not being able to sleep by getting up as early as possible and purposely avoiding naps, no matter how tempted I was to sleep an afternoon away. I'd do anything I could to help ensure a restful night. I drank calming teas and warm milk. I even boiled lettuce and then drank the water because I'd heard that it, too, was soothing. All these things became nightly rituals for me in early sobriety. They not only helped me unwind but also replaced my old unhealthy rituals.

Even so, I still suffered from insomnia the first few months I was clean. I spent my days dreading my nights. When I shared the turmoil I was experiencing with a fellow member of The Program, he pointed out that nobody had ever died from sleep deprivation. I found out that many people had this problem after getting clean. Talking about it helped. **That's how The Fellowship works; one alcoholic/addict supports another.**

Eventually, however, my body decided to catch up on all the sleep I had missed over the years—probably because this sobriety thing was exhausting! So for a while, all I wanted to do was sleep and smoke cigarettes. I would have slept day in and day out if

I could have. Smoking gave me something to do and was something I could anticipate. I wish I could've said that about food instead, but food was very difficult for me to tolerate. It tasted weird and swallowing made me gag. Over time though, my taste buds, like my other senses, began to rejuvenate. Foods were definitely becoming more flavorful, but I just wasn't used to eating regularly and my appetite wasn't that big yet.

During this time, I had lots of new sober friends, and my old friends were still there if I chose to be with them. The first time I'd gotten sober, the counselors at Coldwater Canyon had basically instructed me to avoid my old friends—something I still wasn't willing to do. It had hindered my progress in the past because I felt bad about deserting my old friends to selfishly go and get sober. I promised myself this time that I would still hang with my friends even though I was sober. I wouldn't abandon them this time.

During those first two months of sobriety, I went to parties with my friends and watched them drink and smoke buds (they never did blow in front of me), but I got really bored and irritated by it. Without fail, at these parties, there was always one guy who heard I was getting sober. Inevitably, he would approach me and inform me that he, too, was going to stop using—someday. Then, he would tell me how proud he was of me. Or there were the guys who would laugh at my sobriety. Some even went as far as to bet against me staying sober. "Sketch is trying to get sober? Yeah, right! Sure. That will last a day—at most!" Refusing to succumb to any pressure or ridicule, I felt less and less in touch with these old friends, so I stopped going to their parties.

The time I spent hanging out with new sober friends during and after meetings became more enjoyable and more interesting to me than the time I spent hanging with my old crew. Initially, I thought it was because *I* was becoming boring. How could any self-respecting twenty-two-year-old hang out on a Friday or

Saturday night at a coffee house? That was for dorks! The more attention I paid to the people I was hanging with at the coffee house, however, the cooler I discovered they were. They had a lot more to offer in friendship than my old friends did, or possibly my priorities were changing. Better still, maybe I was growing up.

I realized another gift as more time passed—**I was having a blast staying sober**! Hanging out at all night coffee houses with new sober friends or spending time with them at meetings was more fun than I'd have ever imagined. Honoring commitments at meetings like putting away chairs, washing coffee cups, or sweeping the grounds became a new way of life for me. We swapped a lot of war stories back then, regaling each other with tales of how out of hand and extreme our drug use and related adventures had been. Early in sobriety, it was our only way to connect. Our drug histories were like military medals we wore with pride, or at least I did. The longer I stayed sober, however, the less inclined I was to try to outdo others with stories from the past.

By reveling in stories of my insanity, I was boasting about how amazing it was that I was sober, seeking accolades for how far I'd come. I realized later in sobriety and in life that nobody cares. It is not about who did the most drugs in the past. **What matters is making positive contributions today—in The Program and in society.**

CHAPTER 3
AGE 22 - 23

I wish I could say that beginning to get sober was easy, but it wasn't. There was a lot of work involved. It was mentally grueling. Fortunately, I was not physically going through withdraw too. Serious physical withdrawal can be dangerous and should be medically supervised. For me, however, the physical aspect of getting clean was a lot like recuperating from the flu. I was more aware of my body and of what it wanted and needed. I was exhausted. My appetite and internal clock changed. Stuff like that was moderate compared to what I went through in my head. I was not physically dependent on any of the drugs I was doing, but I was psychologically dependent, and the power of the mind is astounding.

The intellectual fight to suppress the desire to use is incredibly tough and far more challenging than riding out a physical craving. In fact, it is torture. The internal struggle was constant, and the mental anguish was relentless. I felt like smoke should be streaming out of my ears to relieve some of the pressure on my brain. I had an angel sitting on one shoulder, and a devil on the other. They weren't whispering or even yelling at me, they were having an all out fist fight—throwing punches and tackling each other between my ears. The struggle got so wild at times that it, quite literally, broke out of my head. I couldn't contain it. I wanted to use so badly during those moments that I broke things in the house, screamed, and even cried.

Throughout the first two months of my recovery, my emotions boomeranged from total elation about my new life to massive depression and back again. The emotional hangover from swinging between the two poles was very draining. I would have gone crazy if it hadn't been for The Fellowship. The support of the people in the meetings was essential to my continued abstinence, but it was the praying that really got me through. Begging was perhaps a more accurate name for it, but either way, I was down on my knees seeking God's assistance to stay sober. I was so fearful that He would not hear me because of the way I had turned my back on Him when I was intrigued by Satanism. I feared He hadn't forgiven me my past evils.

I was afraid God would let me down because I had disappointed Him so many times in the past—as if He was holding a grudge against me. It's ironic; I pleaded with Him so many times when I was less deserving of His mercy and always expected Him to be there, which, of course, He was. Yet, here I was doing something beneficial and worthwhile, and I was worried that He wouldn't help me. I'll never understand why I doubted God's love and support during that time. I have since learned that He has already forgiven me for my mistakes I have made or will make. I've learned that **God loves us no matter what and will never turn away from helping us and being with us. Once I was truly ready, I am convinced that God was responsible for removing my obsession with drugs**.

It was during these early struggles to stay sober that I noticed one of the many wonderful gifts The Fellowship has to offer. In AA, everyone rallies around a newcomer to help that person stay sober and feel welcome. The people in The Program that I met always made themselves available and really went out of their way to offer me their services and friendship. To this day, I have never experienced as much love and compassion anywhere as I have in the rooms of Alcoholics Anonymous. Nor have I ever felt such an immediate connection and such strong bonds as those that exist in The Fellowship. **There is simply a kinship in The Program that is unlike any other.** I assume the recovering addicts bond together just as survivors of a catastrophe who must join forces or perish; they feel for each other and bond quickly out of necessary.

During this time, I felt very judgmental of others. I compared my drug use to the stories that others in The Program told at meetings. I always felt like my use was worse than the use others described at meetings. I thought that it was easier for everyone else to stay sober than it was for me. I often thought to myself, "You guys are a bunch of amateurs! You're all rookies at drug use!" Eventually though, as I heard more and more stories, I realized that my assumptions about these people were entirely false. There were many people in The Fellowship whose drug use surpassed mine and whose conduct had been even more deplorable than my own. I finally realized that **it did not matter who had the most horrific tale to tell. Each of us has our own tolerance to drugs and our own threshold for pain. We all did as much as we had to do to get us to commit to sobriety.** Furthermore, just because I might have done more drugs than the guy sitting next to me at a meeting **did not necessarily mean I suffered more pain than him as a result.**

If we are lucky, we addicts, eventually, get to that place where we want sobriety. **What finally gets us there is immaterial.** It doesn't matter whether it's a bottle, a straw, a pipe, or a needle that brings us to our knees. The only reason The Program and getting sober worked for me is because I finally wanted the help, and I was finally willing to ask for it. The old adage is true, "When the student is ready, the teacher will appear." The "teacher" may be The Program itself, this book, a family member, an internal whisper, or a dream. When you are ready, you will know the party is over. Each of us gets it when we get it—when it's "our" time and not a moment sooner.

If you are not ready to quit, nothing else matters. I am convinced that *you* have to be done with drugs and alcohol to attain sobriety. You can't just quit because parents, significant others, family members, or friends want you to quit. You may know that you need to quit, and you may respect the evidence pointing to that fact, but knowing it and "being done" are two very different things. You may sincerely promise to stop a thousand times, but unless you're done, you'll break every one of those promises. I know, because I did.

The difference between my final attempt at sobriety and those before was that when I was finally ready, **I was willing to do whatever it took to stay sober.** I wanted it so badly that I gave the same determination to staying sobriety that I had given to getting loaded. **My primary goal was, and still is, to stay sober—no matter what!** I would ask myself daily, "How bad do I want this? Am I willing to do whatever it takes?" The answer was always a confident, "Yes!" I knew I did not have another choice if I wanted any chance of regaining and ultimately maintaining my sanity. I needed to remind myself of this fact *daily*—sometimes hourly. I also knew from previous attempts at getting sober that members in The Fellowship suggested calling another member for support before picking up a drink or drug. Unfortunately, I knew from the past that this did not work for me. This is great in theory. However, I knew that if I wanted to use, I was going to use! The last person I was going to call was another sober alcoholic! This is why I attended meetings every single day. I was so afraid I was going to be hit with the compulsion to get high, and I was afraid that if I did, nothing would stop me. With every passing day that I stayed sober, I distanced myself further from the hold drugs had on me and from my old drug-using friends. I no longer felt comfortable around them.

The craving for drugs began to lessen—something I never could have imagined. In the beginning, I thought about using hourly. Slowly the urge subsided, and then I only thought about it daily. Every time I denied the desire to use, I got stronger and the desire grew weaker. I recognized that it wasn't a need at all—just a desire, an old, very familiar desire. I certainly longed for the familiar, but eventually, I was able to go weeks, then months, without even considering drugs. This was the best gift sobriety ever gave me. **I began to feel free again.**

As time passed, I gained a new perspective. I began to clearly see all the ways my drug use had destroyed my life: the people I had hurt, the lying, the cheating, the stealing, the broken promises, and my ruined health at the age of twenty-two. I had been a prisoner, a slave, to my addiction. I finally came out of denial about how addiction had destroyed my life. It finally hit me—I'd been wasting my life.

It took constant vigilance for me to break free. The suggestions outlined in the book *Alcoholics Anonymous*—the Twelve Steps—were absolutely mandatory for me. To me, these guidelines constituted the meat and potatoes of getting and staying sober. Without them, I might have found some reprieve from my drug use just by hanging out in meetings and with others in The Fellowship, but I feel confident that I would not have found continuous and long-term sobriety without working The Twelve Steps. Most importantly, I would not have found peace of mind, body, and soul without actually doing the work suggested.

First, I had to admit defeat. **I had to admit my total and utter lack of ability to control any aspect of my drug use.** To admit complete defeat was difficult, and honestly, examining all of the miserable events that had taken place in my life was sobering (no pun intended), but I had to do it. I knew, beyond a shadow of a doubt, that if I had to do this on my own, I was a dead man walking. With the AA Program, The Fellowship and, most importantly, my conscious contact with God, I had a chance. **I totally surrendered and put all my faith into everything The Program offered and suggested.**

Following the Steps demanded that I really look at myself honestly. My entire personality had to be evaluated. I dredged up all my fear, resentment, jealousy, selfishness, greed, envy, and every other character defect I possessed. I carefully identified my flaws and reviewed them. With the help of my sponsor and my contact with God, we identified my past faults. I needed to come to peace with my atrocious past and forgive myself. I recognized that I was a mess and that I had definitely made a mess of my life with my drug use. I took responsibility for my mistakes. I realized I had a chance to change and that part of that change included committing myself to God. With God's assistance, I knew I could be a better, more loving and honest person. **I could stop making the mistakes I had made in the past and start living the life I was intended to live.**

I also became aware of the moments in my life that were *not* in my control and that were largely related to other people's actions. To keep my sobriety, I had to make peace with those situations too. Life events of this nature included the physical abuse I suffered at Dad's hands, the babysitter taking advantage of me and other things like that for which I was not responsible. I had to accept that I was powerless over them, let them go, and choose to not let those types of things eat at me anymore, even when I had a "justifiable" resentment or when something legitimately unjust had happened to me. This was *very difficult* for me to do and still is. But when I first embarked on this journey of recovery, someone told me that **I do not have the luxury of having any resentment—however justifiable. And, "To get even, is to *get even worse*."** Alcoholics Anonymous (also called "The Big Book") says, "Resentment is the number one offender. It kills more alcoholics (and drug addicts!) than anything else." I knew I wasn't the exception to that rule.

Once I had completed this personal inventory, it was time for me to clean up the wreckage of my past, which included making amends—financial and otherwise. It was time to address the guilt I carried for the terrible things I'd done and the pain I had caused others. Otherwise, my sponsor reminded me, I would likely use again. I was not willing to take that chance. And so **I made amends to everyone.** As incredibly uncomfortable as this was, it was also incredibly freeing.

When I completed all of this work, I felt totally free from my past and ready to start a whole new life. I felt as though I had a clean slate, a chance for a new beginning. For the first time, I really believed I was going to stay sober. **I was convinced that this twelve-step stuff really worked.** I knew then that this was more than just a temporary break from drugs and alcohol. I was clean and sober and confident that I could remain that way.

One of many gifts that sobriety has given me is the freedom to go wherever I want and do whatever I want. It's been amazing! After the completion of The Steps, I felt as though I could do anything. I relished this new freedom, and this freedom stirred the desire to begin achieving all of my dreams and aspirations. **I knew that if I could stay sober, I could do anything!**

CHAPTER 4
AGE 23

After a few months of sobriety living in LA, I headed back up to San Luis Obispo. It seemed right to go back and finish what I'd started at Cuesta Community College. My first year at that college had been a joke, sadly, at my mom's expense. I stayed sober during my time up at Cuesta College, which was incredibly difficult. For awhile, I did not know a single sober person in that town. Everyone I knew there was a college student, and I was known all around the area as a total partier. In this atmosphere, my new sober way of living was very lonely and depressing.

The Fellowship of AA in San Luis Obispo was vastly and painfully different than the one I'd grown accustomed to in LA. The meetings I attended in San Luis Obispo were often depressing, which was the last thing I needed. Members actually argued with each other. It was disappointing. If I had not experienced The Fellowship in LA prior to returning to San Luis Obispo, I don't know if I could have stayed sober. The Fellowship and meetings in LA were social, fun, loving, and hip. AA describes itself as a "program of attraction, not promotion." In Los Angeles, I was attracted to the people who were members of AA and that attraction was a huge contributing factor to my continued attendance at meetings and to my sobriety.

While I was attending meetings in San Luis Obispo, I was fortunate enough to meet a man named Dave who had thirty-eight years of sobriety. Dave was in his mid-to-late seventies, and I learned a lot from him, although, at the time, I was not yet ready for some of his lessons. Some of what he tried to teach me wouldn't hit home until years later. One such lesson was that life is fleeting, and that the little things that we often take for granted are what really matter most. I wasn't ready to learn that lesson at the time.

Dave and I were having dinner one Friday night at a local Denny's Restaurant. It was pouring rain outside, and I was very depressed because all my friends were out partying, and I was hanging out with an older man at a Denny's on a Friday night. I shared this with him. "Rob," he said to me in a very serene tone, "Today I sat in my favorite chair in my living room and opened a Sprite. I sat in my chair while slowly drinking my favorite drink and watching the rain fall upon the tree outside of my house. As I did, I thought to myself, 'Life doesn't get any better than this!' **It is the simplest things in life that you really come to appreciate**."

I stared at Dave in disbelief, thinking to myself, "Are you kidding me? Please take me outside and hang me now! What do you mean, 'It doesn't get any better than this?' In my opinion, it does not get any more messed up than this—I'm hanging out on a rainy Friday night with an old man at Denny's!" Years later, I finally understood Dave's wise observation. Some of my most beautiful memories consist of brief, simple life moments. It is a wonderful lesson I would never have learned drunk or high.

* * *

I am the man I am today largely because of the men and women I have met and learned from in Alcoholics Anonymous. I love The Fellowship and the people in it, but as I experienced in San Luis Obispo, it's not all sunshine and roses. Not everyone you meet is friendly, good-hearted, or honest inside or outside of the rooms of

AA. I've met some of the most wonderful and loving people in The Program. Unfortunately, I have met some real jerks, too.

After finishing my first semester at Cuesta College, I moved back to LA to finish courses at Santa Monica Community College. I desperately wanted to be back in LA for the high quality Fellowship meetings there. Ironically, it was while attending these "high quality" meetings that I learned that not everyone in The Fellowship is sincere. I was hanging out with some guys, all of whom had been sober longer than I had. They seemed like good people who shared my goals. Actually their agenda was entirely different, and it caught me completely unaware. They ripped off me, my parents, and our neighbors. They were stealing cash from me at the club, checks from my parents and anything they could get their hands on from the neighbors—sober!

When a mutual friend informed me of what these guys were doing, I was enraged, deeply disappointed, and emotionally wounded. I immediately wrapped The Fellowship, The Program, and all the people in it up in one big package, and I was ready to throw it all away. Liars and thieves were participating in a program based on principles like honesty and brotherly love. I determined that it was obviously a bunch of bullshit. Disillusioned, I almost got loaded over it. Luckily, I was able to grab hold of positive memories of visits to the rehab facility and attendance at meetings and of the wonderful people I'd met at both of these places. I focused on the relationships I'd formed with the trustworthy people I'd met, rather than on those who'd betrayed me. Most of the friends I'd made were trustworthy. There was no denying that the love and support I'd gotten from them was genuine. I anchored myself in the belief that I had met some bad people, who just happened to be in The Program at that time. They were not the face of The Fellowship or The Program—they were just people *in* it. I also realized that if their behavior persisted, they were unlikely to stay in The Program long anyway.

I also needed to remember that not all people receive the gift of sobriety. Not everyone who attends meetings gets to live a sober life that is based on the principles of The Program and the design for living that it teaches. Some are only able to stay dry, which is a far cry from recovery. We call those unfortunates "dry drunks." Sobriety is defined as sane, reasonable, rational thinking. That state doesn't come from just not using; it comes from genuine change. And then there are those who don't make it at all. They can't stay away from the booze and bindle. I'd characterize the guys who ripped me off as that type. This almost made me feel sorry for them. Almost.

These guys were business partners in my first entrepreneurial endeavor. We tried to create a sober nightclub. We thought it was the perfect solution for the dozens of young people in sobriety. We would all hang out late at night and have tons of fun. It was difficult for us, however, to find cool places to hang out. For young and not so young sober people, there really were not many places to go, especially late at night.

So one night in October, these friends and I started a sober party at a restaurant. We called it Sober Fest. It was awesome! Hundreds of people from all over LA County showed up. We had a blast. We discovered afterwards that, although it hadn't been our intention, we'd made a profit from the event. Needless to say, we weren't disappointed.

The success of the party and the added incentive of financial gain galvanized us into action. We planned and executed several more events, each grander than the last. We made more and more money as the events we promoted and hosted got bigger and better. We even gave free passes to dozens of people in recovery houses. In addition to the monetary gain, it felt great to give hundreds of young people a fun, sober place to hang out.

After several successful events, I found out that two of the guys who had been planning the events with me had been stealing hundreds of dollars each night from our events. Once I found out, our partnership and friendship ended. It wasn't long before these two guys got arrested for breaking into their neighbor's apartment. Shortly after catching these guys stealing, some other friends and I decided to move the club to its' own location in Culver City. I invested all of the money I'd earned from the previous events in Westwood into the restoration of the property where we planned to have the new club. Unfortunately, after making this investment, I found out that the owner of the property no longer held the permits required to hold events on the premises. He had ripped me off too. I was emotionally and financially devastated! Without permits, the club was short-lived. And there was no way for me to get a return on my investment. Every penny I earned was lost in the restoration and advertising of this new sober club.

In an attempt to save the club, I appealed to the City of Culver, requesting a waiver from the city with the support of members from M.A.D.D. (Mothers Against Drunk Driving), The Claire Foundation, and another rehab center. We implored the City Council to allow us to continue with our mission to provide a sober hangout for young adults and teens. It was such a worthwhile cause, but Culver City denied us, nonetheless. It was a crushing blow that disappoints me to this day.

Even so, the place was rocking while it lasted. It was called Zero Tolerance because we had zero tolerance for drugs or alcohol. Our tag line was "It is not prohibition, it is your decision." We sold hats, t-shirts, and sweatshirts with the club name and our tag line on them. People could be seen all over wearing Zero Tolerance gear. On our opening night, we had over three hundred people show up, some pulling up in limos. The club had it all. There were three cappuccino bars inside, a beanbag room with black lights and a rooftop deck for skyline viewing. We had famous DJs, professional pole dancers, laser light shows—everything, except drugs and alcohol! I was so bummed when it ended.

CHAPTER 5
AGE 23

This series of setbacks—being betrayed by guys in The Program, having to close the club, losing all my money, and losing my girlfriend—were extremely disappointing and depressing for me, but when I lost my sponsee, it was devastating. Lowe, a newcomer to The Program that I had been taking through The Steps, relapsed and subsequently hung himself. He was an African American kid from the Louisiana 'hood, who spoke street slang with a southern drawl. He was only five foot two, but he was solid as a rock. He had a tough demeanor that was highlighted by his missing front teeth and the handmade tattoos all over his body.

Just before Lowe hung himself, he told me the story of how he'd "slipped." He was in downtown LA copping crack from a dealer, and he ended up staying and partying with this guy and his girlfriend for several days. The dealer left for a few hours, and Lowe and the dealer's girlfriend started having sex. When the guy returned, the door was locked, and he could hear Lowe and his girlfriend having sex on the other side of it. He, of course, pounded on the door. Lowe, fearing this guy would kill him, grabbed a knife and hid behind the door. The moment the door opened, Lowe jumped out from behind it and started stabbing the dealer. Then he ran. He didn't know whether the guy lived or died.

I was stunned when Lowe told me this story, and I didn't know if I should believe him. I had no idea what to say or what advice to give him. I wondered if he or I should call the authorities. I didn't know what to say. A day later, he hung himself. I was in a total blur of sadness and shock for weeks afterwards.

Later I was sitting with my friend, Stellio, discussing how depressed and terribly sad I was about everything, especially Lowe's suicide. And then, halfway through this conversation, I had an epiphany. I thought, "**I have a choice here. I am sober, and I can control the way I feel about this and any situation.**" I had never had that freedom of choice before. In the past, my feelings were at the mercy of the drugs; I was unable to control my thinking. Now, being sober, I could. This is one of the biggest blessings sobriety has given me. Awed and inspired, my thoughts raced. "I can let these things destroy me, or I can pick myself up and move on. My thoughts and the way I act on them are my choice. I am not a slave to a drug that controls them. I am free to control my feelings and that is a gift of sobriety and God. If I do not take control of them, but instead, allow them to control me, then I am refusing to receive one of the many gifts The Program and God have given me! I realized I do not have control over people, places, or things, but I most certainly do have control over how I feel about them and what I do about them."

And just like that, I became empowered. I realized that I have a lot of power—the power of choice. **I could let this beat me, or I could get over it. I could have this response to all my challenges.** From that moment, **I chose to be the master of my emotions**. That choice became a great strength for me and a significant part of my character. It carried me through many difficult times and gave me the fortitude to overcome a lot of the obstacles I encountered later in my life, both professionally and personally. I believe all things happen for a reason. **I also believe we become stronger as people through the challenges and disappointments we overcome.**

I am not sure why Lowe died, but I do believe it happened for a reason. Furthermore, I understand that, although I don't know what challenges the future may hold for me, I do know there will be a reason behind each one of them. Maybe I need to learn more acceptance, or maybe I need more practice trusting that something better will happen to me later. I have come to believe that it is all part of God's master plan for my life.

CHAPTER 6
AGE 23

At eight months sober, I learned another important lesson about my recovery. One evening, while I was still attending college courses, I was anxious about taking a big exam the next day and, therefore, was having a hard time falling asleep. Innocently, I asked Mom if she had a Valium I could take to help me sleep. She did and I took it. Later the next day, after my test, I was on my way over to Adam's condo when it hit me. I was driving along, feeling stoked with myself for having eight months of continuous sobriety, when I suddenly remembered the Valium from the night before! What did that mean? Had I slipped? Uncertainty and frustration flooded me. As soon as I got to Adam's, I shared with everyone there what I'd done and why. I wanted each one of their opinions on whether or not taking a Valium for the reason I did was considered a slip or not.

Adam, John, and Mike were there, and they all knew me from my drug-using days. They were also familiar with The Program because they'd all been in it. Two of them, Adam and John, were still using at the time, but Mike was five years sober. Adam and John said I was crazy. "Of course it wasn't a slip!" they said. "Who only takes one Valium?" Mike, on the other hand, said it absolutely was a slip. I was even more confused. As soon as I got back to Mom's house, I called my sponsor Stuart. I had to know what his thoughts were on the matter. The advice he gave me probably saved my life.

I was pretty convinced he was going to tell me I'd slipped. So, anticipating the news that I'd blown my recovery time, my mouth was already watering for the taste of the alcohol in my parents' liquor cabinet that I had every intention of swigging if it was true. There was no way I was going to give up all my time over one lousy Valium. If I was going to have to give up eight months for a slip, then it was going to be a good one, and I was going to get stupidly drunk. I paced the floor as I dialed Stuart's number, ready to get hammered as soon as he told me I'd slipped. Seriously, my plan was to get the news from him, tell him I would call him right back, and stomp over to the bottles and start guzzling. I told Stuart my story, and in response, he asked me some really important questions.

"Did you take the Valium to get high?"

"Well, no," I replied.

He continued, "Did you take Valium in the past to get high?"

"Yes, but I never stopped at just one," I responded, pacing around the room, holding the phone firmly to my ear.

"Was the Valium prescribed to you?"

"No."

Stuart continued, "Would you ever take a single toke off a joint or a single blast of blow?"

Without hesitation I said, "No."

"If you did, would you consider that a slip?" he asked patiently.

"Absolutely!" I exclaimed fervently.

He implored, "Then what, if any, was the difference here?" I admitted Stuart's line of questioning was totally valid. And after considering what he said for a moment, I explained that justifying the medical use of Valium, which hadn't even crossed my mind, wasn't the point. Yes, I took it as it is prescribed by doctors, but that was not the crux of my dilemma. I was distressed because the Valium wasn't prescribed to me. I agreed with Stuart that my intentions were honest, but then reminded him that, under the circumstances, my actions could be considered a slip. It was a totally gray area. If Stuart agreed that it was a slip, I knew I would use again. I could feel my thirst for my first drink increasing.

Sensing my conclusions, Stuart changed the course of the conversation. He said that this decision was mine. He suggested that the final decision be between God and me. This stumped me completely. Stuart suggested that I give it thirty days. He told me to take my time, pray about it, and just let it sit with me for a while to see how it felt. I didn't need to introduce myself as a newcomer in the meantime. If I decided that I had slipped, then I would lose my sobriety time and be back within my first thirty days. His advice stopped me and my cravings cold. I couldn't get drunk because if I hadn't already lost my sobriety, then I didn't want to lose it. Stuart's advice undeniably prevented me from going on a drug run that may have never ended. It was the most amazing and surprising advice I have ever received. That conversation unquestionably saved me from getting high that day. Heeding his advice, over the next few days, I changed my mind several times. One day, I decided I had slipped, and the next day, I decided I hadn't, and so on. With each new verdict, I called Stuart. After numerous phone calls, he calmly reminded me that we were waiting for thirty days before making a final decision.

I shared my circumstances with hundreds of sober members at dozens of meetings over that thirty-day period. There was no consensus. I received a variety of opinions ranging from strong convictions to nonchalance and indifference. Some thought it was a slip, absolutely. Others said it definitely wasn't. Most people weren't adamant about it. And then, there were those, like me, who flat out didn't know.

At the end of the thirty-day waiting period, I made my decision, and I was totally secure with it. When I had taken that single

Valium, as prescribed, with no intention of getting high, I had not slipped. My resolution was steadfast, until just before I celebrated my first year of continuous sobriety. As the day approached, my faith in the decision began to falter.

CHAPTER 7
AGE 23

I was looking forward to accepting my one-year cake at a birthday meeting, which is a really big deal in The Program. I woke up one morning with a weird dream. My friend Adam was staying with me at the time, and I shared the dream with him. In it, I was in The Program, but I was secretly getting high. No one knew but Adam, and I was screaming at Adam that he better not tell anyone because I was about to get my one-year cake, and I didn't want to miss that experience because, after so many attempts at sobriety, I had never celebrated that one year mark.

    Adam thought it was just a weird dream and told me not to read too much into it. I, however, thought a lot more about it. I wondered what it meant. I realized that I had been feeling increasingly uncomfortable in the past few weeks. I hadn't been able to figure out why, either. I knew I was excited about coming up on my one-year birthday, but why, at the same time, was I pissed off at everyone and everything? The distress I was feeling about my dream and my constant state of agitation compelled me to take a closer look at the situation. With that in mind, I did as The Program suggests; I picked up a pen and paper and started writing.

    Without forethought, I started writing a letter addressed to God. My pen flowed quickly and easily across the paper as I sought answers about what was disturbing me. I didn't have to write long because after just a few sentences, the answer came. I was uncomfortable getting a cake for my one-year birthday because of that Valium. Something inside me didn't feel right about it. I felt somehow "unclean" because of it. Funny, but that incident hadn't crossed my mind since I'd settled it a few months back, but I knew then that I hadn't resolved it after all. It loomed before me yet again.

I shared with Adam my conclusion from my writing. He didn't agree with it. He thought I was totally clean in my sobriety and that I ought to be celebrating my first year by taking a cake. After careful consideration, my gut told me that I had to be accountable for that damned Valium. Regardless of my intentions, a doctor hadn't prescribed it to me, and I had taken it anyway. I had to count the day after I'd taken it as my first day of sobriety. That meant wiping out eight solid months of hard work and clean time just like that. It also meant no cake, no birthday, and no celebration. It was so disheartening.

I had been all fired up and exhilarated about my first year of sobriety. To have been so close and then to see it slip into the future like that was incredibly deflating. It had been seven years since my first attempt at sobriety, and I still hadn't reached the one-year mark. I wanted that one-year anniversary so badly! I also felt like I deserved it. However, I also knew that being *rigorously* honest in all my affairs, especially whether or not I'd taken a drug, was absolutely paramount to my continued recovery.

So I erased the eight months of time. Doing so was bittersweet. Part of me was sad and disappointed, but a larger part felt free. I had a clear conscience and no longer had to worry about being haunted by that Valium. If I ever felt a little "dirty" about it, it would not matter because the success of my future sobriety would not be based on that decision.

This experience taught me that my **sobriety is not so much about quantity as it is about quality**. Of course, continuous sobriety is incredibly important. As I accumulated consecutive days and eventually years of sobriety, I was doing what was necessary to stay sober and to receive all the gifts of sobriety and The Program. But when I sacrificed eight months of sobriety time for the sake of my integrity, I improved the quality, if not the quantity, of my sobriety. My recovery is more about how well I'm living each day rather than about how many days I've put together.

* * *

I was able to replace the time I'd surrendered by staying sober for another eight months, and when I finally celebrated my one-year birthday, I was so proud of myself! I had such a great feeling of accomplishment! I was on such a sober high—it was amazing! Then, the next day came. The emotional letdown was one hundred times worse than the let down after a regular birthday! The exuberance of finally achieving one year of sobriety after seven years of trying faded quickly. At first, I'd been a part of The Program on and off, failing over and over again, and then, I had finally committed to recovering and had persevered. After reaching this landmark goal, I couldn't help thinking, "Now what?"

Despite the letdown, I did not lose the lesson. The high of my celebration, followed by the low of the day after, reminded me that **staying sober happens one *day at a time!*** I have thus far been able to stay sober through everything life has thrown my way and **staying sober continues to be the greatest accomplishment of my life**. Without my sobriety, I do not have a chance of creating anything in my life other than problems and misery. A life of using drugs will lead to death, institutions, jail, or a living hell. **A life of sobriety allows me the freedom to create and live the life of my dreams.**

The setback on my path to sobriety taught me a lot of valuable lessons. The friends who ripped me off taught me that not everyone in The Fellowship is a saint. Although our nightclub, Zero Tolerance, was financially profitable and certainly entertaining, it was also exhausting. I spent late nights running the club and the majority of my days promoting it. It was physically and mentally draining. Shutting down the club, metaphorically, closed one door in my life, allowing another door to open. With that business venture behind me, I was forced to look for a new source of income. Losing all the money in that investment taught me that I can lose money and still remain sober and happy! I also learned an invaluable business lesson about risk. I learned that I could lose money and still make it back, sometimes a hundred times over. Losing my girlfriend showed me that **I could walk through heartache without picking up a drink or a drug**. It taught me that I could hurt emotionally and *feel* it. I didn't have to numb the pain or obliterate a memory or anything else melodramatic. I simply lived to see another day—sober. And again, I trusted that there was something better in store for me. My experience with Lowe taught me to value life. It also made me even more appreciative of my own sobriety. Getting and staying sober is painful and difficult. Watching Lowe struggle and fail made me realize what a blessed achievement my sobriety is. With Lowe's passing, **I truly recognized my sobriety for the precious gift that it is**. We don't all get it. But for those of us who do, it is a miracle.

After learning some of these hard lessons and feeling very empowered by them, it seemed time to move forward. I said farewell to the loyal friends who were a part of the nightclub scene with me: Jason, Adam, Kelly, Shane, Stellio, Brett, Eric, and Jared. They'd been honest, great friends and had nothing to do with the thievery. My friends Brett, Jason, and Kelly are no longer alive. Jason was hit by a car and killed. Kelly died of liver failure due to alcoholism. Jared recently informed me that Brett died. Eric is still using. At the time of this book's writing, Adam had just celebrated two years of sobriety after fifteen years of trying. I lost touch with Shane and Stellio, though I know Shane became a contestant on the TV show *Survivor*. Jared became an actor and rock star. The guys who ripped me off ended up doing a lot of jail time.

* * *

I had continued to attend school at Santa Monica Community College while starting the nightclub. I finished a two-year degree, which included courses in real estate. For me, real estate was exciting. When I began my nightclub venture, I certainly couldn't know if it would be successful, though it did look very promising. However, I later realized that the closure of Zero Tolerance was a sign. After that venture, I focused my attention on real estate, where, as Fate would have it, I would make my mark.

CHAPTER 8
AGE 24

Staying sober was my first priority and real estate became my second. I loved the limitless financial opportunity it offered. In real estate, you get what you put in. I had applied the same fervency to my sobriety that I had exhibited in my drug use. I shifted that passion and determination to fuel my new career. Real estate is better than selling vacuums door-to-door—which, yes, I tried. I say *tried* because I never actually sold one, but I did spend a month trying to sell Kirby Vacuums door-to-door while living in San Luis Obispo. The only other sales-related jobs I'd ever held were in retail stores. I'd worked as a front desk clerk in a hotel. I'd been a dishwasher, a busboy, and a waiter. I also delivered pizzas for awhile, and I'd had my share of blue-collar jobs too—working as a digger at a construction site, laying cables for a small phone company, and setting up and breaking down jumps for horses in an equestrian show. That was my cumulative life's work, excluding dealing, which, unfortunately, brought in the best money. I failed miserably at each of these jobs, usually within a couple of months. My using, of course, prevented me from becoming a valued employee.

    I embarked on my real estate career with many misconceptions. Primarily, I was under the impression that the industry had an unsavory reputation, and perhaps in some circles, it does, but the truth is that Realtors serve the public in a way that positively impacts lives and communities. Real estate agents help people realize their dream of owning a home. They also help families make moves that often positively affect their lives. I have a better understanding of the incredible service I bring to people's lives now, and it has definitely changed my own opinion of the job. Initially, however, I didn't see going into residential real estate as a step up in the business world that made sense for me. I was extremely adept in the night club world, but I had virtually no business acumen or practical skills appropriate to the traditional business world. None of my previous work experience had prepared me for what I would undertake as a real estate agent.

My initial clumsiness and ineptitude in the business world now seems comical to me. My lack of knowledge was apparent. For instance, I did not know how to use a computer. Seriously, I didn't even know how to turn one on. For that matter, I couldn't balance a checkbook, and it took me hours to type a single letter. So, for over a year, I typed each letter out with an old-fashioned typewriter. I remember the days I spent typing dozens of boilerplate letters, hen-pecking the keys with my pointer fingers, and using correcting fluid to fix the errors. It was painful, and it took me nearly an entire day just to mail out half a dozen letters.

At the time, I lived in Santa Monica with Eric, whose mom owned the apartment building. He didn't have to pay rent and only charged me five hundred a month for the extra room, which he used for spending money. Another friend, Matt, slept on the couch. It was a great setup until clients needed to call me at home. Cell phones were uncommon and very expensive then, and I did not have one. So, whenever I would get a business call from a potential client, Eric or Matt would answer in their lazy gangster slang, "Yo, what up?" To make matters worse, there was usually music blasting in the background. It was totally inappropriate for business and did nothing to instill trust in prospective clientele. I had to get out of there. To complicate the situation further, Matt started getting heavily involved with a local Venice gang, which meant he was selling blow, carrying a gun, and that people were stopping by at all hours. Matt's dealing was really what motivated me to get out, but Monica, my girlfriend at the time, facilitated it. She wanted me to move in with her. Finally, she and I found a place in Venice.

Monica and I were beyond broke. We lived in a little one-bedroom apartment, and our rent was $895 per month. Each month, we barely made enough money to cover it. We struggled just to buy food, gas, and other necessities—like cigarettes. I spent less on food than smokes. We'd search in the couch cushions and under the seats in our cars, hoping to find quarters instead of pennies. There was a diner nearby that served eggs and two pancakes for $1.99. Lunch there was just $3.99. I ate there every single day for almost a year. It was part of my routine. The frustration over our financial situation created a lot of tension between us, and we fought a lot.

In those days, my daily grind began at the office at nine-thirty. I would type out all my letters until early afternoon, and around one, I'd take a break for lunch. I was only good until about two, so after lunch every day, I was ready to go home. I'd head back to our apartment, feeling totally discouraged and beaten, get out of my clothes, and lay on a beanbag chair in my boxer shorts with the blinds drawn. I sat in complete darkness like that every afternoon, watching porn movies and smoking cigarettes. I was in a total rut. Depressed, I wondered what I was doing with my life. I felt like a total loser! I knew I could not get high, but I could not get much lower either. I found out what depression feels like sober, and it sucked!

Months and months went by like that. Then, it happened. I met my first client! I was taking "floor time," meaning that I was taking calls that randomly came into the office. These clients were a husband and wife who were moving to Los Angeles so that the wife, Mrs. Tardio, could get into the entertainment business. I wound up leasing them a house in Venice. It was my first paycheck! I was so stoked! I only made about nine hundred dollars, but the amount didn't matter. The fact that I made *something* was thrilling! I remember this couple fondly. Years later, Mrs. Tardio's surname changed from Tardio to Leoni—Tea Leoni. Funny how life connects people. I still see her today. We now live in the same neighborhood and our kids attend the same school. I am eternally grateful to Tea Leoni for unknowingly giving me the confidence that jump-started my career.

CHAPTER 9
AGE 24 - 26

I was grateful to secure my first lease. I wish I could say that, from that point on, everything just got easier and money began to flow in like water, but it did not. However, staying sober did get easier. **Sobriety became a way of life for me.** I no longer considered getting high an option. This is one of the many unexpected blessings I have received in sobriety. I assumed I would *always* struggle to stay sober. But I no longer have to struggle. As long as I stay close to The Fellowship, keep my spiritual connection to God and act and think daily in the ways that helped me get sober, I can remain free of the obsession—free of the struggle that was once all I knew.

My new challenge was how to make a living. I did manage to secure a few more leases that year, and each one yielded a similar commission. My entire gross income for the first year was a whopping $3,500. It was ugly. I was often not able to pay my share of the expenses, so the fights with Monica continued and escalated. As a last resort, we brought in a roommate to help make ends meet. We let the new roommate have the bedroom, and Monica and I partitioned off a portion of the living room for ourselves by hanging a sheet for privacy. It might have been easier to tolerate our makeshift, tight quarters if the neighborhood had not been as shoddy as the apartment. We often woke up to find homeless people crashed on our front stoop. Thieves also broke into both our cars and our storage unit. It was an absolute drag, and we were very unhappy there.

Venice was not the place to be in 1992. The Rodney King riots were taking place, and we literally had the National Guard posted at our front gate. Tanks rolled down the inlet streets and along Venice boardwalk. In retrospect, it was exciting to be part of the madness and chaos, but I am thankful that my life is not like that today.

My living situation was challenging, but my personal appearance was my greatest professional hindrance. I was young, but I looked even younger than I was. Prospective clients and colleagues were always asking about my age—and experience. I might have been twenty-four, but I scarcely looked old enough to drive a car. It was a huge disadvantage.

My car was also a problem. I drove a red Mitsubishi Mirage with surf racks. It was adorned with surf shop, reggae, and Grateful Dead stickers. Brightly colored Mexican blankets covered the cigarette burns in the backseat, and the gas cap was missing. A rag was stuffed into the opening of the gas tank. I lost so many gas caps at gas stations, and eventually, I just couldn't afford to replace them anymore. I can hardly believe I used to chauffeur clients around town in this car or that people were brave enough to get into my car at all.

I still had bleached white buzz-cut hair, a goatee, and earrings. The look had been advantageous as an event planner and nightclub manager, but it was a drawback in the business community of Los Angeles. My dress shoes were Doc Martins, and I wore ill-fitting second-hand suits. Monica brought them home from the photo shoots she worked on, and they were often too tight, too long, or too baggy. On occasion, I'd be in a jacket so tight I couldn't sit down with it on and still breathe. It was such a sight to see me in front of a client trying to casually and gracefully get out of the jacket before getting into my red surfer mobile so I could drive them around to find their dream home. It is no surprise that I never sold a house.

The fact that I wasn't able to contribute toward any expenses seemed to outweigh everything else in my relationship with Monica. She'd had it, and she let me and everyone else know about it one afternoon while I was eating at the diner I frequented. She stormed in while I was in the middle of my meal and started yelling at me in front of all the other customers and the wait staff, most of whom I knew fairly well. Her verbal onslaught was sudden and severe. I stared in stunned silence, fork in hand. She screamed at me, "You're a fucking loser and a child!" She continued yelling at me for several minutes. This would have been hurtful enough in private, but it was incredibly embarrassing being berated like that in the place I ate every day. Monica enumerated my faults. She accused me of being incapable of taking care of a woman and raged about what a little boy she thought I was. Then, she demanded to know why I didn't get off my ass and go get a job. She declared that I would never amount to anything in real estate. Her tirade ended with, "Who do you think you're going to be, Donald Trump?" I sat at the counter, speechless, still holding a forkful of food in mid-air. Having satisfied her anger, she turned and stomped out of the diner. After she left, a man came up to me and said empathetically, "If that was my woman, I would have hit her!" I appreciated the sentiment and, although I would never hit a woman, I agreed that her behavior was totally out of line. Her immature outburst was humiliating. Frustrated and hurt, my eyes welled up, but I fought back the tears. Monica was right about one thing. I *was* still a child, but I was definitely not a loser.

* * *

With Monica behind me, I had no idea what lie ahead. I didn't have many options. With a heavy heart and a humble spirit, I moved back in with Mom and Sam. This move turned out to be a triumphant blessing. Once again, I learned that nothing happens by mistake, and that there are no coincidences. She and Sam were renting a house in Pacific Palisades, and one of their neighbors, Judith, happened to be a real estate agent. We both worked for the same real estate company, in different offices. I worked in the Venice/Marina Del Rey office, and she was the training director in the Palisades office. Judith convinced me to transfer to Pacific Palisades and work under her guidance. It was a perfectly legitimate reason to leave Venice altogether and an opportunity to thrive under the tutelage of an experienced agent!

Within the first two months in the Palisades office, I was on the verge of selling my first house. Finally! After a year and a half of hard work and dozens of rentals, I was going to make my first sale. I was ecstatic! Unfortunately, my victory was short-lived. The sale never closed escrow. The buyer changed her mind. It was an unfortunate turn of events. I'd worked so hard for my first sale, and I felt it was well-deserved and long overdue. I refused to succumb to self-pity, accepted the situation as a minor setback and persisted. I would also attempt to comfort myself by believing this was all happening for a reason and in God's master plan. Much to my dismay, a series of canceled escrows followed. Five sales in a row opened and canceled. It was mental and financial torture!

I was forlorn and frustrated. I couldn't take it anymore. I was disappointed and insecure, and I found myself in my manager's office admitting defeat. My manager, Fred McMillan, shared a story with me. He asked me if I knew who the greatest baseball hitter of all time was. I replied, "Babe Ruth." Shaking his head in disapproval, he announced, "Ted Williams." Fred passionately elaborated, "Ted Williams had the highest batting average of all time. His career batting average was just over .300. Ted Williams was the best hitter in baseball. That means that for every ten times he was at bat, he hit the ball only three times. That means that seventy percent of the time, he struck out, and he is still the best! Rob," he said sincerely, "You have a hit coming!"

I lifted my head from my hands and looked at him with tears streaming down my cheeks. I tried to respond with enthusiasm, but I had no confidence at all, so the best I could muster was, "Okay, I guess I can do it."

Still trying to boost my morale, Fred vigorously agreed, "Of course you can!" Then he escorted me out of his office so he could go sell a house.

A month or so later, I got my hit. I sold and closed my first deal. After almost two years in the business, I finally got my home run. In fact, I *kept* hitting home runs. I sold several houses in a row! I found that I was steadily selling homes. Experiencing uncertainty and self-doubt taught me a valuable lesson. **I could not allow the experience of failure to convince me that *I* was a failure.** Barbara De Angelis, Ph. D., a motivational speaker who has inspired me over the years puts it this way, "**It is not who you are, it is who you are becoming, that matters. This is where the dance of life really begins.**"

By the end of my second year in real estate, I'd made $28,000. In my mind, I was a player! I was so proud of myself. I could barely keep from kissing myself in the mirror! Once I had a little bit of money, I left my parents' house and rented a one-bedroom apartment in the Palisades on Sunset Boulevard. It was $895 per month. Once I moved into my own place, I became a total workaholic, devoted to working every day and driven by fear of not being able to afford my rent. That was all I did—work, work, and work! I did not go out with friends or on dates because I did not have any money. I would work from six in the morning until six at night, go to an AA meeting, then go back to the office for another hour or two. That was my life for the next two years, and it was fine with me. I was determined to get my career off the ground.

An author I admire, Brian Tracey, likens launching a new

enterprise to a plane taking off. He says, "Like a plane, any business that wants to get off the ground must give all of its energy at the beginning to get off the ground. Later, when it is off and flying, you can turn on the automatic pilot." Back then, I was still on the runway, but I was rapidly picking up speed, and I was definitely prepared for take-off. But just before I got my business plane off the ground, I had a wonderful experience with faith.

* * *

One night, while lying on the dirty, garage sale couch in my one-bedroom apartment, I was feeling depressed about how I was going to pay my rent and make my car payment. I generally felt doomed. But suddenly, I felt a sense of peace and security—a feeling of well-being settled around me like someone had just covered me with a blanket. In that moment, I knew that God would take care of me. I might not still be able to pay my rent or make my car payment. Okay, so those things would go, but **I was sober and no one could take that from me.** I had control over my feelings and thoughts. And I believed God had not brought me as far as He had just so that He could drop me on my ass. Worst case scenario, I would sleep on friends' couches. I had made dozens of friends in AA, and any of them would lend me their couches and their support. This feeling of faith, of certainty that all would work out the way it was supposed to, put me at total ease. Moments later, I got up and went back to the office to get some stuff done. I went to my mail slot at the office and there was an envelope inside. I almost fell over when I saw what was inside—a check for $3,500. It was a referral fee from another agent. I had referred my grandmother to him in Florida. She'd sold her condo with this agent's help, and I had forgotten that I would receive a referral fee for it. I had chills from the shock. The experience changed my life and made my faith in God bulletproof.

CHAPTER 10
AGE 26 - 28

Emboldened by my stronger faith, I took my first real risk in business; I hired an assistant. His name was Jesus. He was in his early twenties, and he was an awesome person. This was a leap of faith for me because, at the time, my annual income was only $28,000. Jesus was half African American and half Hispanic. He was absolutely one of the nicest guys I had ever met, but he was not always the best assistant. He did the best he could though, and at the time, he was perfect for me. The two of us learned the business together. What Jesus did not know, however, was that I couldn't afford him. I was constantly afraid there wouldn't be enough money to go around, and I was always worried about how I was going to pay him. Invariably, each month, I struggled to pay his salary, but I always did. I paid him before I paid myself. Of course, then I worried about how to pay myself.

I looked around at all the real estate seminars I attended and at the brokerage community in general and noticed that all the top producers had assistants. That was not the reason I hired one though. I could truly see the need for one in my office, and I knew how beneficial having one would be. I needed to free myself from the endless clerical work involved in real estate. I saw that my time would be better spent in the field, prospecting for new clients. I believed that hiring an assistant was a good move, and indeed, an assistant turned out to be a great investment. My income more than tripled the following year.

* * *

I made $88,000 in my third year in real estate, and as far as I was concerned, I was wealthy. I didn't know what to do with the money. In fact, just knowing I had so much money made me feel really awkward. I was accustomed to struggle and disappointment. I was used to doing without, and I did it well. Suddenly, I could afford things. I did not know how to deal with success.

Gradually, I adapted to my new circumstances. It was one of the more pleasant adjustments I've had to make in my life. Little by little, I bought myself a thing or two. Eventually, I got rid of the Mitsubishi Mirage and bought a Ford Explorer. I had always wanted an Explorer. I had told all my friends that it was my dream car. I informed everyone that *someday* I would be able to afford one. The desire to own that car consumed me, and for that reason, it was inevitable that it would someday become a reality. The day I got my new Explorer was one of the most magical days of my life.

I also bought a few new suits, off the rack, for $200 dollars each. Certainly that was not extravagant, but I mention the suits because they represented significant personal progress for me. I'll never forget how I felt wearing hand-me-down suits that didn't fit right. I was grateful to have them at all, but it was a challenge to wear them and feel good about myself. Before I shopped for suits off the rack, I went to garage sales, not retail stores, to find suits. I remember one day in particular, back when I was broke. I stopped at a garage sale in Brentwood because I'd noticed two suits on display. They were the nicest suits I had ever seen. One was Hugo Boss and the other was a Giorgio Armani. I tried them both on and they both fit, kind of. I was able to get in and out of the jackets without looking like I was struggling to get out of a straightjacket. I had no idea how much suits like these cost, but I imagined it must be a lot. Tentatively, I approached the woman hosting the sale and asked her what she wanted for them, wholly prepared to be dismayed. She responded, "Four for each or three each if you take both." I was crushed. There was no way I could afford six hundred dollars.

So, in my typical garage sale mode, I attempted to negotiate. I pointed out the flaws in both suits. The woman acquiesced, "Okay, I will sell them both to you for five dollars." I went into a mental spin. It was like I was in a movie and everything was warped I heard her words in slow motion, "Five dollars." I freaked inside with excitement. That whole time, I'd thought we were talking about hundreds! I put on my best poker face and calmly repeated, "Five dollars." She nodded. I couldn't believe it. "Okay, I think that's fair." It was all I could do to not run to my car to get my wallet. When I handed her the money, I was afraid she was going to laugh in my face and say, "Oh, I'm sorry, did you think I said five 'dollars'? You idiot! Anyone would know these suits are worth far more than that!" Elated, I was almost in tears when I drove away. I wouldn't look behind me when I pulled away, fearful she'd wave me back to correct her error. I drove directly to my apartment, excited to try the suits on again and strut around in front of the mirror looking like a big shot in my garage sale suits!

* * *

My plane was finally in the air. My career was quickly gaining elevation. I wasn't yet ready to level off and turn on the autopilot, but when the opportunity presented itself to do something other than work, I took it. I made $150,000 my fourth year in real estate and was earning at least as much in my fifth year when a friend of mine named Jason asked me to go out with his girlfriend's best friend. It would be a double date to celebrate this girl's birthday. I surprised my friend and myself by agreeing. All I ever did was work. But this time, for whatever reason, I agreed to take this girl out for her birthday. Two years later, the birthday girl became my wife. I was twenty-six years old, and by the time I turned thirty-two, Jill and I had divorced.

While I was married to Jill, I learned how to think rich. Jill came from a family with money, so because of her background, she *only* thought rich. I was exactly the opposite. I had a poverty mentality because I'd been broke my whole life, and my mindset hadn't changed just because I had money. I always denied myself luxuries, saying things like, "That is how *those* rich people live. That's for them, not you." I routinely prevented myself from enjoying my financial success.

I used to drag Jill into all my bargain basement shopping places. She would cringe, watching in embarrassed amazement as I bargained with retail sales clerks. She finally pulled me aside and said, "Rob, stop acting like a pauper. You are not a pauper. And what's more, you are catering to high-end clientele, and you need to look the part. You need to look like a high-end salesperson." Reluctantly, I started buying nicer suits, shirts, and ties from Neiman Marcus (which I used to call "Needless Mark-ups") in Beverly Hills. At the time, I didn't believe I deserved to be wearing nice expensive clothes. Again, "That was for *those* rich people."

Early in my marriage and still somewhat early in my career, I started thinking like someone who expects the best. **I now believe we all deserve the best of what life has to offer.** I also believe you need to start thinking rich in order to become rich. Some people don't believe this, and I think that's what stands in their way. I once heard, "You have to believe it to achieve it," and I knew instantly that it was true. Once my mindset had changed, I started bringing more money into my life through sales.

My relationship with Jill also offered me the opportunity to think like a man. Jill had a six-year-old daughter, Ellis, who became my stepdaughter. Being a father to Ellis catapulted me into being a mature, responsible adult. I started thinking like a man, husband, and father. At the age of twenty-seven, I was no longer a kid. Things changed rapidly after my marriage to Jill. Nothing illustrates the astounding advancements in my life more vividly than an amazing coincidence that happened while Jill and I were married. We were house shopping, which, for me, was an incredible feat in and of itself, and we happened to take a look at a place in Brentwood that was on the market. We didn't end up buying that particular house, but when Jill and I were standing on the sidewalk out front, I recognized it and got chills. I started laughing and at the same time became a bit choked up. I said to Jill, "This is the same house that had the garage sale where I bought those two nice suits for five dollars!" Wow, had things progressed! I used to buy their hand-me-down suits, and now we were considering buying their home.

The ending of my relationship with Jill also taught me another great lesson. **I can stay sober through difficult life events.** At one time during the divorce, I became incredibly angry. In fact, it was probably the angriest I had ever been in my life. Without drugs or alcohol to numb my feelings, I had to experience my feelings full force. I remember yelling to my sponsor about my anger. I wanted to stop feeling, even if it was for only an hour. I wanted to step out of my skin, get out of my head, and not have to *feel* the venom that was running through me.

The first question my sponsor asked me was, "Are you thinking of getting loaded?" To my amazement, I fired back, "NO!" **Getting high was not an option, and, more significantly, I did not even have the urge.** This was a profound moment for me. **I truly felt recovered from my addiction.** I realized that I could *feel* this angry and not have to go out and get high over it. Although it was a wonderful realization, it didn't help me feel any less angry. My sponsor then gave me a suggested assignment that, at the time, I did not want to accept. He wanted me to pray for Jill. He wanted me to pray that her every wish would come true. Furthermore, I was to wish for her every wish I had for myself. In addition, I was to say the prayer of Saint Francis morning, noon, and night until my anger abated—even if that meant I said the prayer all day long.

At first I would scream this prayer out loud, and I did not mean a word of it. Days passed, and I started to calmly say the prayer, though I still did not mean a word of it. A week or so went by before I began to *feel* the words of the prayer and the meaning of what I was praying for. Once I did, the magic happened. I found peace in my heart.

The Prayer of Saint Francis

Lord, make me a channel of thy peace;
that where there is hatred, I may bring love;
that where there is wrong,
    I may bring the spirit of forgiveness;
that where there is discord, I may bring harmony;
that where there is error, I may bring truth;
that where there is doubt, I may bring faith;
that where there is despair, I may bring hope;
that where there are shadows, I may bring light;
that where there is sadness, I may bring joy.
Lord, grant that I may seek rather to comfort
    than to be comforted;
to understand, than to be understood;
to love, than to be loved.
For it is by self-forgetting that one finds.
It is by forgiving that one is forgiven.
It is by dying that one awakens to eternal life.
Amen.

CHAPTER 11
AGE 28 - 29

In the early days of my recovery, I often heard that "more would be revealed" later. As with so many other things in my life, the meaning behind those words would unfold slowly. Initially, I thought it meant simply that my memory would get better and that I would recollect things along the way, but that wasn't it entirely. It also meant that as we grow and mature in sobriety, we are confronted with issues that we might not have been prepared to handle previously. We are presented with problems as we become capable of solving them.

I was driving to my office one morning, listening to the radio, humming along to a song by 10,000 Maniacs that I'd heard many times before. The song was called "What's the Matter Here?" and although I'd heard it before, that morning I really heard the message. The song is about a woman sitting in her apartment listening to her neighbor beat his son in the apartment next door. I pulled my car over to the side of the road and broke down in tears. A huge rush of emotions poured out of me—anger, frustration, sadness, and even the fear I experienced as a child while hiding from Dad. I hated him with every fiber of my being at that moment. He beat me and abandoned me, repeatedly. All of that pain was still with me, and it was time to let it go.

The lyrics of the song reached me that day because it was time to forgive him and make peace with my past. I cried that morning until I couldn't cry anymore. In my car, totally drained and in awe of the feelings that the song provoked, I knew what I needed to do. Until that morning, I thought I had released these feelings when working The Steps with my sponsor. As I sat in my car, I realized I still had more work to do and that this was the beginning. I was ready to embark on a mission of forgiveness. Although I didn't realize it at the time, this mission would also include an opportunity to make my amends.

Sitting in the car crying, I also recalled the time, during my late teens, when I was trying to stop using and get off the streets and had requested financial support from my parents. Mom didn't have the money. At the time, Dad had the money, and he flat out rejected me. I can't blame him, given my track record, but his refusal still hurt. Worse still, he had told me he needed to concentrate his efforts and money on his new step kids.

A bit surprised and angered by his statement, I had reminded him that I was his firstborn boy, named after him, and that his two step kids were only eight and twelve and had only been in his life for a matter of months. He told me that it did not matter because he only made smart investments, and that I was not one of those investments. He only invested in winners, and I was a loser. I was flabbergasted. I retorted that if that was his position (and he repeated that it was) then as far as I was concerned, I was an orphan!

During this confrontation, he was sitting behind his desk and Brett and I were sitting next to each other across from him. Dad didn't respond to me. Instead, he looked at Brett and yelled, "If you don't get Rob out of here, I will reach across this desk and snap his fucking little neck!" I left his office with tears in my eyes.

I saw him five years later. He showed up unexpectedly and uninvited at Brett's wedding. I spent no more than ten minutes with him that afternoon. He told me he was happy that I was doing well. I was sober, in early recovery, and dating Monica. He said he would like it if we could reconnect. Naturally, I was excited by the possibility but experience had taught me well, and I was more hesitant and doubtful than anything. He called me a few weeks later to discuss an investment deal he thought I might be interested in. I didn't have a dime to my name at the time and told him as much. Once he knew I was unable to invest, he said he'd call me the next time he was in Los Angeles. And once again, he disappeared from my life. That was it. I hadn't heard from him since then. The sum total of my experiences with Dad had landed me there at the side of the road—bawling.

Once the gut-wrenching sobs subsided, I took a deep breath and finally acknowledged how much pain I was holding onto about my relationship with him. Thanks to other members of The Program sharing their wisdom with me, and what I'd learned from reading dozens of self-help books, I knew what I needed to do. I had a deep emotional wound that needed my attention. I needed to take action to facilitate healing. **Forgiveness is essential to maintaining peaceful sobriety.** Others may have wronged and mistreated me in the past, but **the only way for me to find peace and happiness in my future was to let it go by forgiving entirely.**

Days later, I decided to call a therapist. Over the next several months, my therapist was able to help me make peace with my very tumultuous past. We talked through countless injustices and unsettled scores. With a combination of heartfelt discussions and soul soothing meditations, she made it possible for me to let go of the lingering resentments I harbored towards Dad and others, even if I felt they were justified. After putting in three to four months of hard work with her, I was able to ultimately break free from those resentments.

Around this time, I was also attending a real estate seminar based on some of the philosophies we were also discussing in my therapy. Mike Ferry was the seminar's speaker, and he was fabulous. I owe a lot of my business and personal success to what I learned from him. Ferry challenged us to hurdle over our own personal obstacles and enthusiastically championed us to apply his emancipating philosophy of "G.O.I"—Get Over It—to those things in our lives that were preventing us from being free and living our dreams.

Ferry's presentation was provocative. As he talked, I thought about all the things that I was holding on to in my own life: Dad's abuse, Mom's deference to Dad, their mishandling of the divorce, the babysitter's perversions, the mistakes I'd made, the years I'd lost to drugs, my guilt at having turned my back on God, and injustices galore. So many things were bogging me down. I thought to myself after hearing Mike, "I am sick and tired of holding on to this stuff! Get over it, Rob! Grow up! Move on! I am bigger, better, and stronger than these things!" After years of internal torment, I was finally able to let go. And by doing so, I became the person that I am today. I decided that if I could survive all that, then I could take on anything. Bring it on!

Initially, I did not realize that Ferry was actually directing us toward forgiveness. Letting go allows forgiveness and gives us the true ability to move past an injustice. **What does not kill us makes us stronger. Each event needs to take place to support the next event in life.** Each experience, which I no longer identify as good or bad, prepares me for the next experience that life has offer.

* * *

I look back on my drug-using years and thank God that I did not get everything I wanted—like bigger bags of better drugs. If I had, I would be dead. So if not getting what I wanted was ultimately better for me back then, I'm sure it still applies today too.

I believe that God's master plan for me is far greater than anything I could plan for myself.

My belief in that master plan was reaffirmed when, after I'd complete my therapy and made some evolutionary changes as a result of Ferry's seminar, Dad called. It had been approximately six months since my emotional curbside catharsis, compliments of 10,000 Maniacs. Dad told me he had terminal cancer. I was speechless. I did not know how to react. A part of me was sad for him, but the rest of me didn't know what to feel. My immediate reaction wasn't my best moment. I blurted out, "So, this is what it takes to get a phone call from you?" He was instantly defensive and said, "This is probably not the time to go over all of that." I agreed and asked about his prognosis. He said the doctors hadn't been definitive about his life expectancy and that there was still some hope he could beat the cancer with chemotherapy sessions. We talked about his efforts toward recovery and the realities of what was happening to him.

I visited him a few times over the next year. The first time I saw him, he looked like I remembered him—larger than life, handsome, and powerful. He was still the football player, the military man, the lawyer, and my dad. We spent some time during those visits catching up on life. He repented for not being much of a father, and I accepted his apology. I made amends for being a menace in his life, and he accepted my apology. My dad did not earn my respect during the time we spent together that year, but he did earn my love. Our visits with each other were very loving and forgiving.

The most important aspect of our time together was that he finally allowed me to be his son. He was never a true "dad," but I was, at least, able to be a "son." It helped us both heal because I was able to act lovingly toward him. I released my resentments and forgave him. In continuing this forgiveness process, I was reminded of all the people who had forgiven me, especially Mom.

The fact that these loved ones could forgive my bad behavior allowed me to forgive myself.

Dad did the best he could, and I did the best I could. He certainly did not live up to my expectations of him as a father, and I realized that I did not live up to his expectations as a son. But he did all he could, and how could I hate him for that? I don't anymore. I no longer hold him, or anyone else, accountable for the way I experience life today. Taking the Mike Ferry's harsh advice, I moved forward. I'm very grateful that I did.

* * *

In subsequent visits, I watched Dad grow more and more frail. The cancer reduced him to a battered, skinny old man. He was living alone in a small apartment in Roseville, California, and he spent his time in a La-Z-Boy chair watching a television that was propped up on a cardboard box. The saddest part about all of this was the lack of people in his life. At the time I was not speaking with my brother Brett. Only three people visited him with any regularity: me, one friend he had from college, and one he had made at a local restaurant he frequented. He had no other friends and no other family. He'd been abandoned by everyone—even the family that he had made such a big deal of supporting financially. Empathetic, I never asked where they were. I assumed those relationships were irreparably damaged, and I didn't want to pry.

The second to last time I saw him, I checked him into an assisted living facility where he spent his final days. I am happy that I was there for him as a friend and a son. It was a melancholy time. I sincerely felt sorry for him because of the reality he had created with his choices. I was able to replace the anger and resentment I had held onto for so many years with compassion and pity.

My last visit with him was unscheduled. The nurse called me

at home and told me that he'd been sent to the hospital. He wasn't expected to live much longer. I caught the first flight out of Los Angeles International Airport. In the end, I wanted to be there for him. I paused before entering his room, trying to prepare myself. I found my barely recognizable father lying in a hospital bed. I couldn't tell if he recognized me, so I sat down on a chair next to his bed. I spent the last day of his life at his bedside. He could no longer speak, so we sat in silence. Searching his face for any signs, I followed his gaze to the window. As we watched the wind rustle the leaves of the lone tree outside, I wondered what he was thinking. He probably wasn't wishing he was at his office trying to make another dollar. Despite all his efforts, he was completely broke in the end. He'd actually gone into hock, pawning his jewelry and valuables for cash. I thought, perhaps, in his last moments, that he might be wishing he was sitting beneath a tree outside his hospital window enjoying the gentle caress of the breeze on his face.

The moments shared with Dad at his deathbed were tremendously sad and profound. This is when I started really paying attention to the little things in life. I realized that what Dave had tried to tell me years ago was true **"The little things do matter most."** My father's death transformed me, and out of that transformation, a new awareness was born. I became more alive inside. I was already enjoying life, but I began to appreciate it even more deeply. I intended to maintain this hyper-awareness and to always be present in the moment, living every moment to the fullest, but the routines of life can interfere, and I often need to be reminded of that commitment.

One of the most vivid reminders came to me as I sat on a surf board. I was surfing a break called Cloudbreak in Tavarua, Fiji with my friend, James. He was next to me in the lineup when he caught me gazing off at the horizon. He knew exactly where my mind was when he asked, "Are you at the office?" Shocking me back to the present and a little ashamed, I admitted that I was. I was surfing one of the best breaks in the world, and I wasn't in the moment—an egregious affront to our surfing philosophy. Then James said something that really reached me. He declared, "**Rob, life is not a dress rehearsal!**" As I listened to James, the decision I had made in Dad's hospital room pounded in my head like the waves on the reef. **Thank goodness for life's little reminders and for friends who help us along the way.**

CHAPTER 12
AGES 28 - 30

In the early years of my real estate success, I worked long hard hours. My day began at 4:20 a.m.—not 4:30 or 4:45. I woke up each day promptly at 4:20. I got up with enough time to pray, stretch, make coffee, and get to the gym by 5:00 a.m. I worked out at the gym for an hour while listening to self-help books on tape, then took a steam bath, showered, shaved, and got dressed in time to be at the 7:00 a.m. Palisades AA meeting. If I arrived at the meeting early, I'd sit in my car and read my daily positive affirmations aloud or rehearse my sales scripts. My day ended at 6:00 or 7:00 p.m. each day, six days a week. I heard Mike Ferry say at a seminar, "The morning is the sling shot to the rest of your day." I had mastered my mornings—I was militant about my schedule and nothing interfered with my day.

Dr. Stephen Covey's books introduced me to the concept of an Integrity Account. Just like making withdrawals and deposits in a bank account, we invest and spend from our Integrity Account. Every time I make a commitment and keep that commitment, I make a deposit into that account. Every time I break a promise, I make a withdrawal. For instance, if I tell myself I am going to get up early the next day and go to the gym and I follow through, I contribute to my Integrity Account. If I do not go to the gym, then I withdraw from my Integrity Account. The more deposits I make, the bigger the account—resulting in higher self-esteem, self-worth, and self-confidence. The more I withdraw from the account, the lower my integrity.

I believe I unconsciously started playing the Integrity Account game in early sobriety. My Integrity Account benefited the longer I stayed sober. I have Dr. Covey to thank for providing me with the tools to hone my abilities and help others. I play this game all the time. I consciously enrich my life and career every time I honor my agreements.

* * *

I solicited business like a mad man. Each day, I prospected for new business. I made cold calls and knocked on the doors of local residents. I was not satisfied unless I spoke to at least fifty new prospective real estate leads. It was tough and humbling. Soliciting business on the front lines comes with a lot of obstacles. Phone calls ended before I could finish my introduction, doors slammed in my face, and occasionally an irate homeowner screamed me right off their front porch and out into the street. I was constantly faced with rejection. Mohammad Ali inspired me to persevere. Before he became a world-class athlete, he would tell himself, **"Today I will suffer in order to live like a champion tomorrow."** My personal mantra was simple. I believed that I had no other choice. **If I wanted success, I had to go out and work for it!** And I did.

At one time, my office manager informed me that my relentless prospecting was making the other agents in the office uncomfortable. The agents felt my non-traditional tactics reflected poorly on our office's public image. I explained to my office manager that **complacency or mediocrity was not an option for me**. I believed my unconventional methods were the only way I had a real chance of generating any business. My passion led me to create another daily mantra, **"Do what others won't, to

achieve what others won't."

Discipline did not come naturally or easily to me at first. Admitting this to myself, I sought advice and assistance. Guided by the desire to have an amazing and prosperous life, I employed Mike Ferry and his company to coach me for a number of years. They held me accountable each and every day. I recorded all of my activities and submitted them for review. This disciplined schedule contributed to my ability to run my business like a business. As a student of Mike Ferry, I knew exactly how many contacts I needed to generate enough leads, how many leads I needed to generate enough appointments, how many appointments I needed to make to get signed contracts, and how many signed contracts I needed to have to close an escrow.

The last year I recorded my daily activities, I spoke to 9,760 *new* people over the course of the year. In addition to the nearly ten thousand new contacts, I made follow-up calls and numerous appointments. Soliciting new business took phenomenal effort. Sometimes it took six or seven attempts to make one contact. I estimate that I made thirty thousand cold calls, referral phone calls, or door-to-door contacts *each* year. The work ethic I employed and the schedule I adhered to made me feel impatient around people who complained about their job being too tough or who whined that their life was not fair. At a meeting, I once heard a sober friend say, **"Thank God life is not fair, because if it were, I would be dead or in jail."** Recalling this simple statement comforted and motivated me hundreds of times when I wanted to complain about injustices. I could have looked at my past as unfair and continued to fail because of previous mistakes, but I chose not to. Instead, I would live by the words of Mike Ferry and, "Get over it!" and thank my lucky stars that life was *not* fair.

Later, I teamed up with an affirmation and accountability partner, which proved to be of immeasurable worth. Bill and I called each other every morning at 5:00 a.m., just before I arrived at the gym. In my car, on the phone, we yelled our positive affirmations at each other. Yes—yelled! I know this sounds incredibly dorky, but it pumped me up for the entire day. In addition to shouting at each other every morning, we held each other accountable for the weekly goals we set for ourselves. On Mondays, we set and shared our goals, and then each Friday, we discussed our progress or lack of progress towards accomplishing those goals. I directly attribute two achievements in particular to those accountability calls.

Consistently frustrated by the amount of time I had to spend reading, I decided that I would take a speed-reading course. I voiced this goal to Bill, but it was one of those things I kept procrastinating. Bill cleverly forced me to take the class. Weeks had passed since I'd set the goal, and each Friday, I failed to report any speed-reading progress. I wasn't even enrolled in the class when Bill asked me if pain or reward motivated me. Anthony Robbins' courses had taught us that people are either motivated by pain/consequences or gain/reward. Consequences motivated me. Bill asked, "Is there anyone you don't like?"

I replied, "Yes, I can think of someone."

Delighted, he replied, "Good." He instructed me to send him a check for five hundred dollars made out to this individual. If I did not complete the course by the date he and I agreed to, he was going to mail the check. I made sure to complete the course in time!

One Monday, I declared to Bill that I wanted to help with a charity event. It was important to me to give something back. **The Alcoholics Anonymous program had worked wonders in my life, and I had wholeheartedly committed to applying all of the principles in every aspect of my life.** The twelfth step in The Program is the principle of service and helping others. This was during the time Jill and I were married and our family was about to increase by one. Jill and I were about to have our son, Skyler. As a stepfather and soon-to-be birth father, I was primarily interested in a charity that benefited children.

I became involved with a Spinal Muscular Atrophy (SMA) charity. The first SMA and Habitat for Humanity fundraising event I co-sponsored was a golf tournament at the Malibu Country Club. The next three events were tennis tournaments at the Pacific Palisades Riviera Country Club. Once the events were well established, I handed the responsibility over to a woman more closely affiliated with SMA This allowed me to concentrate my efforts on supporting another charity called Chrysalis. I sponsored two more tennis tournaments for the new charity. During this time, I also contributed my time and money to their Butterfly Ball Committee. The funds raised for these charities, plus my donations, totaled more than I thought I could earn in a year, let alone donate.

These philanthropic efforts filled me with joy and pride. **Thanks to the AA program, numerous motivational guides, and my affirmation partner, I began to truly realize my potential.**

CHAPTER 13
AGE 31 - 39

My income continued to increase by leaps and bounds. It surprised me and made me a little uncomfortable. I was unaccustomed to this kind of success. When my income jumped to half a million dollars in one year, I was certain it was a mistake. How could I bring home so much money in one year? I doubted my success, never feeling I was entitled to make that much money. It was way too much for me. It made me really nervous and self-conscious. I imagined that my friends and the brokerage community thought I was conceited and that I was acting like someone I was not—some "rich" person.

Unfortunately, to some extent, there was some truth behind my fears. A lot of acquaintances and even some family members seemed to be bitter about my newfound success. People began talking negatively about me. At first, I let it affect me and was very hurt and upset. Eventually though, I refused to let their gossip impede my growth. I turned the negative energy into a positive force. Empowered, I repeated, "**I control the way I feel about myself, and I will not allow my feelings to be manipulated by how others feel about me.**" I have learned that if you choose to become successful, your relationships with people you thought were your friends may end; don't worry about it. You will gain new relationships with individuals on a similar path to success. You will exchange depleting relationships for enriching ones.

For the longest time, I labored to change the opinions of the gossip mongers. I engaged them in debates. I argued that some successful people struggled harder than the average person. Their misconceptions used to really frustrate me. I discovered that it was more socially acceptable to complain about struggles and misfortune than it was to share stories of success. Although everyone wants to achieve, true financial success is met with animosity. Those who succeed are accused of showing off. Why is that? Envy? I know I was often frustrated as I struggled in the beginning, and I remember feeling a little envious of prosperous people. To overcome this feeling, **I began releasing thoughts of envy and, instead, chose to be inspired by others' successes**. Shortly after this perceptional shift, I began to prosper. Was it a coincidence? Perhaps, but I don't think so.

Similarly, my assessment of successful, corrupt people altered. I used to think that it was unfair that some wealthy people attained success through corrupt and unethical behavior. Believing that these people must be unhappy and that they would certainly later pay the price of bad karma would pacify my anger. Like those people who gossiped about me, I invited negativity into my life because I was being judgmental. When I let go of those feelings of resentment, I determined that I needed to hold myself accountable to my own ethical code. I could choose who I worked with and turn down business opportunities with unethical people. **I am a much happier person when I truly wish others all the blessings and happiness life has to offer**.

I almost allowed all this self-inflicted, unnecessary pressure to get the best of me. This newfound success baffled me. Hardship and disappointment were familiar companions—in fact, we were old friends, but success was new to me. From it, I began to experience new fears that were full of the same old self-doubt and insecurity. What if I couldn't do it again? What if this was the only year that I would make a lot of money? I imagined my peers ridiculing me when I failed, pointing and laughing as they watched me fall. Dread had me in its grip.

Fortunately, I did not give in to my fears. The next year, I again earned $550,000. Each subsequent year, I increased my income. I eventually grossed over one million dollars a year. For someone like me, earning one million dollars in one year seemed like an impossible goal. I was thrilled and grateful. This affluence persisted for several consecutive years, and without realizing it, I began to expect it.

Expectations can be dangerous. In The Program, we're taught to avoid having them. When I took my cash flow for granted, I did not achieve my goals. In 2005, as I wrote this book, I only earned $600,000. After consistently making a million a year, anything less was very disappointing. I know most people would be thrilled with a $600,000 annual income, but for me, it was a misstep. I was upset and embarrassed, and I felt a bit like a failure. Then I recognized that my self-confidence was attached to a material goal. If I was in the spotlight, I felt grand about myself. When I wasn't, I began to feel like a loser.

It was a great lesson for me. Aware of my folly, I embraced the truth that **I am not the income I make. I am a total winner every day that I stay sober and continue to be a kind and loving person to others. The rest is icing on the cake**—and I do not *need* any icing. I like the security, but it is not mandatory to my happiness. **Happiness and the way I feel about myself is within me—not my pocketbook.**

I am still dedicated to my business and to earning a nice income. However, I have learned not to be a slave to money. **I noticed that when I do things for the right reasons and have faith, things always work out the way they're meant to.** It can be challenging to truly let go of those expectations. Sometimes, we must seek mentors to teach us how to free ourselves. I needed help to learn to run my business before my business began to run me, and I needed help running my life and managing expectations.

* * *

I studied books, tapes, and any other material I could get my hands on from mentors knowledgeable in all areas of life. I studied everything from health to wealth to philosophy and spirituality. I created my own tapes, like the one my stepdaughter Ellis recorded with me. She was about eight years old when we recorded it. We read daily affirmations as we played relaxing baroque music in the background. I treasured that tape. Not only was it adorable, but it also motivated me. That tape emphasized accountability in all aspects of my life, especially regarding family. I still strive to improve my life and myself, especially in the areas of health, communication, spirituality, sales, and money.

Every year, my education continues. I absorb knowledge from each mentor, book, tape, seminar, and AA meeting I attend. From keeping my eyes open and learning as much as possible from it all, **I have gained far more than I ever thought was possible in my life.** That does not mean that my path has been easy. I've certainly failed. I've failed at a number of things, both professionally and personally, but failures do not interfere with my sobriety or my overall success. I've unsuccessfully attempted to get other businesses started. I have foolishly invested money. I've solicited business that I didn't get, and I've lost sales that I thought I had. And yet, my philosophy still holds firm. **I believe that everything—both success and failure—happens for a reason.** I learned from each experience, and **every event, success, or failure has prepared me for the next. I appreciate everything that has happened to me in my life, even if I have not enjoyed it, because the totality of it made**

me who I am today. My success was not a mistake, but for a number of years, I thought it was a fluke. I thought I was incredibly lucky. I learned, however, that "luck is the residue of hard work." I worked very hard for what I earned, and I am proud of my accomplishments, but I am also grateful for all of my many blessings.

Most of what I learned, I learned from others. My mentors in life and business guided my success. I used their experiences and advice as a road map to find my own direction. Along the way, I modified some of their ideas to better suit my own internal compass. I adopted what worked for me and discarded what did not. I am truly grateful to those who have shared their experiences, their discoveries, and their wisdom with students like me and to those who will in the future. My experiences taught me that the **road to success is open to anyone**! Yes, even you! *The Law of Attraction* is one of the many invaluable concepts I have incorporated into my life. It states, very basically, that the energy you put out into the world will attract more of the same to you. Therefore, you are responsible for creating your reality and your life. I learned this message by watching a movie called *The Secret*. Please open yourself to receiving the message of *The Secret*. It will add jet fuel to your life! (*The Secret* is available as a DVD, as a book, and as a CD at **www.thesecret.tv**.) The following excerpt is from an e-mail I received from a friend. It paraphrases the message from *The Secret*:

> Asking For What You Want and Co-Creating With The Universe
>
> Most people don't fully realize that we all have within us the ability to co-create our lives with the help of The Universe. So many of us are taught to accept what we are given, to not even dream of anything more. But our hopes and dreams are The Universe whispering to us, planting an idea of what's

possible, while directing us toward the best use of our gifts. The Universe truly wants to give us our heart's desires, but we need to be clear about what they are and ask for them.

To ask for something does not mean to beg or plead from a place of lack or unworthiness. It's like placing an order. We don't need to beg the salesperson for what we want or prove to them that we deserve to have it. It is their job to give us what we ask for. We only have to tell them what we want. Once we have a clear vision of what we desire, we simply step into the silent realm where all possibilities exist and [we need only] let our desires be known. Whatever methods we use to become still, it is important that we find the quiet space between our thoughts.

From that still and quiet place, we can announce our intentions to the pure energy of creation. By imagining all the details from every angle and how it would feel to have it, we design our dreams to our specifications. Similar to the ripples created by a pebble dropped into a pond, the ripples created by our thoughts travel quickly from this place of stillness, echoing out into the world to align and orchestrate all the necessary details to bring our desires into manifestation. Before leaving this wonderful space to come back to the world, release any attachment to the outcome and express gratitude. By doing this daily, we focus our thoughts and our energy, while regularly mingling with the essence that makes it possible to build the life of our dreams.

* * *

The power of the mind is awesome. On my journey toward financial success, the power of suggestion became a substantial tool. When I began my career, I was handed a book written by

Og Mandino called *The Greatest Salesman in the World*. One of Mandino's assignments was to write down my monetary goal. The instructions required me to write down a specific dollar amount. He encouraged his readers to shoot for the stars, even if it made them feel uncomfortable. I selected my number based on my favorite number—eight. As directed, I wrote $88,000. I didn't think I had a chance of making that much money in one year, but I followed the instructions in the book and wrote it down. This assignment made me feel uncomfortable and excited.

After three years of working in real estate, I forgot about that goal, although I believe now that it was embedded in my subconscious. I made exactly $88,000 my third year in real estate. Years later, I pulled the book out of a drawer and reread it. When I saw the figure that I had written down in the book, I got chills and almost cried. When I'd originally written that amount, it had seemed astronomical and unattainable. It was unbelievable that I'd made that exact amount just a few short years later. Even more amazing to me was that the amount was a pittance compared to what I earned the year I reread the book…by then, I was making about $88,000 per month!

Another thing I attribute my success to is my ability to prioritize. I maintain my sobriety, stay close to The Program, and attend lots of AA meetings weekly, am of service when I can be — inside and outside of AA, and take a personal inventory of my behavior at the end of every day. I try to recognize where I might be getting off track and quickly make amends or correct any mistakes. **Keeping conscious contact with God through prayer and meditation is my favorite priority.**

Continuing to live soberly, I expect to live a long life that is 180 degrees of difference from the life I could expect when I was a kid using drugs. In my drug induced youth, I did not care if I lived another day. All I cared about was hitting the pipe or sticking a needle in my arm. Life was meaningless and miserable. **Today,**

my life is full of joy, possibilities, peace, love, happiness— in big and small moments, and prosperity. I have this life because I was able to get sober and stay sober, and I will lose everything if I lose focus on the two forces behind my success: sobriety and a loving God.

CHAPTER 14
AGE 40

Constant vigilance, introspection, and meditation led me to formulate my own philosophy based on eight important areas of life. I call them The Eight Equities: Spiritual, Mental, Physical, Family, Romance, Financial, Career, and Social. I believe all eight are important, and all eight need to be in balance for a happy life to result. This can be achieved when you employ C.A.N.I., an acronym Anthony Robbins created to emphasize "Constant And Never-ending Improvement." Approaching The Eight Equities with dedication and discipline has produced phenomenal results in my life.

Spiritual – On as many days as possible, I spend twenty minutes in the morning and twenty minutes at night in prayer and meditation. This does not include the time I spend reading books on the subject. I am not a part of any organized religion. I treat religious beliefs as schools of thought; I adopt what works for me and discard what does not. By so doing, I have created my own understanding of God that is heavily influenced by the book *Conversations with God* by Neale Donald Walsch. **My connection with God is very strong, and I believe it is the foundation of my sobriety, peace of mind, and happiness.** I rely on God's love and guidance to carry me through all of life's experiences, and I find God's presence reassuring and comforting during the difficult times. My greatest influences regarding prayer and meditation are Dr. Wayne Dyer, Deepak Chopra, Eckhart Tolle, Marianne Williamson, Lama Surya Das, and Marlise Karlin. From them, I have learned the importance of these spiritual tools.

I feel moved to mention that a five-week meditation course with Marlise Karlin, in particular, generated amazing results in my life. Her instruction enabled me to open my heart up as never before. The experience led me back to the woman who is now my wife, Halle. Meditation grounds me and assists me in being a more loving person, something I aspire to be every day.

<u>Mental</u> – Read, read, read, and learn, learn, learn. I constantly study subjects that will help me excel. I study self-help, spiritual, inspirational, financial, and business texts that help me move toward my goals. In my opinion, reading is the best way to learn. I never graduated from high school (although I did obtain my GED) or college. The books I read, the tapes I listen to, and the seminars I attend are my university experience. I regret that I didn't attend more classes in high school and college, and I still have a great thirst for knowledge. **When we are learning, we are growing, and personal gain accompanies growth.**

The Mental element of life must also be balance by how I make my decisions. Early in sobriety, I was told that the real work of sobriety would begin once the drugs and alcohol were out of my body. **To live a peaceful, happy, and sober life, I needed to control my mind because it controls the way I feel about situations.** I was warned that my thinking would sometimes be irrational once I was no longer medicated by drugs and alcohol. This is one of the main reasons newcomers need sponsors. My sponsor was an incredibly helpful guide, not only through The Twelve Steps, but in making a lot of life decisions as well. In early sobriety, I definitely needed that.

Physical – In the immortal words of Buddha, the Hindu Prince Gautama Siddhartha, founder of Buddhism, "Every human being is the author of his own health or disease." A balanced mind and body connection is crucial to a peaceful existence.

Around 1993, I had been clean and sober for almost two years. I decided to quit smoking cigarettes. I smoked a pack a day for ten years and the effects showed. I couldn't walk up a flight of stairs without stopping to catch my breath. People twice my age climbed stairs with ease. It was embarrassing. I thought to myself, "I went through all this to get sober. What a shame it would be to live an unhealthy or shorter life because of the deadly effects of cigarettes." I quit on my twenty-fifth birthday. Shortly after, I decided that I needed to be in better health, my friend Jason gave me a pair of his running shoes, exhibiting *The Law of Attraction*. I could not afford my own. I didn't care that they were a size and a half too big. I started running and paying attention to my diet. I read books on fitness and later, when I could afford it, I worked out with personal trainers. **I strongly recommend that physical fitness be a priority in recovery and in life.** Since 1993, I have kept a close watch on my physical health. I exercise daily, eat healthfully, and do detoxification cleansing. Living a healthy life allows us to enjoy a long life.

Family – Family is different for everyone. It can be a source of strength or torment. I love my extended family, although I am not very close to them. I am, however, close to my immediate family—to Halle, Skyler, Grayson, and to my wife's extended family. My ex-wife Jill and I also maintain a healthy relationship.

Halle, Skyler, Grayson, and I spend our weekends together. In my profession, dedicating weekends to family can be a costly decision. I know I am sacrificing, but the benefits far outweigh the costs. Due to the time-sensitive nature of real estate, as a compromise, I have chosen to be on-call by phone and have surrounded myself with a team of agents that assist our clients during weekends. The joy and satisfaction that I gain by faithfully spending that time with the people I love make me a far richer man than more money ever could. **I learned that making money is not what life is all about. Yes, it's important, but it's not as important as family.**

<u>Romance</u> – Romance is the area of my life where I am the most vulnerable, and where I have made the most mistakes. I imagine that's true for many of us. **I believe relationships are the most challenging, worthwhile, and rewarding life experiences that we have available to us.** As a general rule, members of The Program advise those new to sobriety avoid getting into a new relationship within their first year. I understand why this is recommended, although I did not heed that advice and dated in my first year of sobriety.

The ups and downs of a new romance can be dramatic and confusing, especially if you are just getting sober. Early in recovery, my emotions were all over the place. I was not used to feeling anything, and suddenly, I was feeling everything. I was trying to figure out who I was. **There was no way for me to know what I was looking for in a relationship until I understood more about myself.** In addition to the emotional turmoil, my physical chemistry was changing. My body was struggling to regain its natural balance. I would have been better off not adding the excitement, frustration, and insecurity of a new relationship to the mix.

I learned the hard way with romance. **I feel like a perpetual student when it comes to love.** I wish I could undo the hurt I caused others and myself, but I've accepted that I cannot. I have to believe that it *all* took place for a reason and that those relationships, however painful, prepared me for the woman of my dreams—for my beautiful wife, Halle.

I met Halle in 2004 and, with the exception of a six-month break-up, we've been together ever since. During those six months apart, I learned some things about myself through meditation and self-examination at Marlise Karlin's retreat. I finally accepted that I was the one that needed to change to make our relationship work. It was time for me to start being the understanding and flexible person that I knew I could be. Halle and I exchanged wedding vows in the spring of 2007. Now, I willingly embrace all of our differences. I recognize that they strengthen our love for each other. I am so blessed to share my life with Halle. She taught me how to be a better partner. Her generous, accepting, patient, relaxed, and loving manner inspires me to reciprocate. Her guidance helps me prioritize and focus on one of life's most treasured gifts—an intimate relationship.

<u>Financial</u> – Most people understand the importance of this equity. During a seminar, Mike Ferry once made a humorous and poignant statement that I consider often, "Money does not make people happy, however, I would much rather be unhappy *with* it." After the crowd stopped laughing, he continued, "Seriously," he said, "think about it. There are always happy and unhappy people in the world. **Money does not define who is happy and who isn't.** However, with money, it sure makes it easier to find happiness." I agree, and as a result, I monitor my finances constantly.

I was once on the phone with a good friend of mine who didn't have a dime to his name. He and I were going over his expenses together. He was hoping I might be able to help him find a way out of his financial hole. When I asked him about his expenses, he replied in a frustrated tone that he didn't know what they were. "I'm not good at this stuff," he complained. I leveled with him, "You have to make yourself good at this stuff! How can you possibly improve your finances if you don't even know what they are?" Most people must overcome the same obstacle that impeded my friend's financial stability. I empathize with their anxiety because I once shared those feelings. For the longest time, even in early sobriety, balancing my checkbook was a real challenge for me. But everyone can learn to manage money. **To accumulate wealth, you need to understand how to manage it.**

To stay organized, I developed a system. I break down my expenses into percentages. A broad overview follows:

Living expenses - 30% or less
Taxes - 40% or more
Investments - 10%
Savings - 10%
Charity - 5%
Entertainment - 5%

I review my profit and loss statements every month and my spending habits every quarter. **I want to make sure that I am always living within my means.** For quite awhile, I lived well beneath my means. *The Richest Man in Babylon* taught me the importance of saving money. In the book, George S. Clason recommends, "Watch your pennies, the dollars take care of themselves" and "Be generous, not foolish." There is an abundance of opportunity and money out there just waiting for someone to take it. At first, I had a hard time believing this, but now I realize that it is absolutely true.

Career – I approach each day asking, "What can I accomplish, and how can I give today?" I try to make the most of each day. **Try to live in the present, because you will never get to repeat a day.** When you approach each day with focus, you can accomplish great feats.

One day, early in my career, I was talking with another Realtor after lunch. I shared my plans with him: I aspired to be a top-producing agent. He responded lazily, "I have no desire to be a top producer. I just want to make enough to get by." His response shocked me. Doesn't *everyone* want to be the best they can be? Doesn't *everyone* want to make the most out of themselves? Doesn't *everyone* want to love their job? Doesn't *everyone* want to become massively successful? The answer is no. What makes me happy may not work for someone else. I choose to be passionate and proactive about my career decisions; not everyone makes that choice.

I know that I create whatever success I wish for in my life. That is the best part of all this. *It is entirely up to me, and within me, to create the success I desire.* **We are in charge of our lives! I believe that God's Will grants us the freedom to create the life we have always dreamed of having.**

I would also suggest that you find someone in the industry you want to pursue and ask them for guidance and assistance. Take him or her to lunch and ask questions. You will find that most successful people are more than willing to share their experiences and help others succeed.

Social – As you may have guessed, implementing all of *The Eight Equities* in life is time-consuming, which is why I feel this final equity is significant. It is important to spend time with friends away from work. We need to interact with others. It doesn't matter how you choose to socialize, but it is important to get out and connect. **I feel true friendship is an irreplaceable resource; it fosters ideas, encourages laughter, and benefits the soul.**

* * *

In addition to The Eight Equities, one of the best ways to become successful is to follow the paths of successful people. I followed most of my mentors' suggestions. Here are a few of those ideas that I found helpful.

First, my **mindset determines my success.** I thrive when I believe that it is possible to accomplish what I want. **A positive mindset is easier to maintain when you set goals.** It is difficult to succeed when you don't have goals or a way to measure your success. When I apply *The Law of Attraction*, I must know what I want in my life in order to attract it.

Second, I must have faith that God wishes only good fortune for me. **My job is to take actions that will help initiate the results I want to see and to then leave the rest to God.** I have faith in God's master plan for my life, so I believe that everything will unfold in its own time. I use quiet meditation to tap into that master plan. Deepak Chopra suggests that it is in these quiet and still moments that we allow ourselves to slip into the gap and get in sync with what The Universe wishes to unlock for us. Trusting that God has my back has enabled me to triumph over my biggest obstacle—fear. Mistrust and uncertainty lead to debilitating trepidation, and to avoid that stagnating force, I still must conquer the anxieties that sometimes occupy my head. **I must defeat fear with faith!**

Third, discipline creates order and control in my life. **I must have the willpower to follow through with what I say I am going to do.** Training and self-control builds my confidence and fills my Integrity Account, which fuels me to act. Simply put, you must do something if you want to see results! You can't just talk about your goals and expect your life to change—you must exert yourself. Poet, playwright, and novelist Johann Wolfgang von Goethe put it eloquently when he said, "Thinking is easy, acting is difficult, and to put one's thoughts into action is the most difficult thing in the world." Don't allow fear to keep you from realizing your potential. Everyone faces similar obstacles. I suggest that you meet the challenge head on, embrace each opportunity, and take control of your destiny.

* * *

I would like to share a report written by my most influential mentor, Mike Ferry. The report is titled "Becoming a Self-Made Millionaire." I believe it summarizes a large portion of Part II of this book.

1. Dream big dreams ... all great success and achievements in life begin with a dream of some type ... a vision of some accomplishment ... of something great that you'd like to be or have or do. We have to remember that we have to have a dream if we want a dream to come true. Do you have a dream, even in this economy, of being a self made millionaire?

2. Do what you love to do ... the key to high level success is generating the internal motivation to do what you have to do every single day. It's easier to make this happen when you are doing something that holds your attention ... something you really care about ... something that really interests you or something that has great financial rewards for the work you're doing. A majority of people who fail financially in life fail because they don't like what they do. Normally people without dreams don't love what they do ... dream the big dream so you can fall in love with your work.

3. Focus on your unique strengths ... everybody has certain strengths, what are yours? People who succeed at high levels and make millions get there by

identifying their strengths and then putting all their efforts towards those strengths and taking advantage of them. Each of us has special talents and strengths and the key to our success is identifying and using them daily.

4. See yourself as self-employed ... which is easy for all of us in the Real Estate business because we are. This means you have to take a high degree of responsibility for your actions and your results. We have to look upon everything that happens as though we are the sole cause for making it happen and we will reap the benefits because of those activities. You are your own boss - be a good one.

5. Never consider the possibility of failure ... the fear of failure is always a major reason for the failure that we come across as adults. Self made millionaires are always going to take calculated risks to achieve their goals. Our attitude towards risk-taking is probably the most important indicator of whether we're going to be wealthy or not. There's no security in the Real Estate industry only opportunity. When you're confronted with a risky situation ask yourself, "What is the worst that can happen if I do this now" ... and make sure that doesn't happen.

6. Develop a clear sense of direction ... you've all heard the statement, "People don't plan to fail, they fail to plan". Each of us has to have a direct road map that leads us to what we want and then we have to go after it every single day.

7. Work hard ... everybody who's worth a tremendous amount of money has put in a tremendous amount of

energy and works hard. People work eight hours a day to make a living and everything over that eight hours determines their level of success. People who are wealthy are putting in at least sixty hours of work every week and they do it because they enjoy it.

8. Hang around the right people ... people who succeed make it a habit of spending time with other positive success-oriented people. They carefully avoid negative people and negative conversations and are always looking for people who can help and they can help in return.

9. Teachable and coachable ... most self made millionaires have average intelligence. Most did very poorly in school and therefore never became impressed with their own intelligence as, unfortunately, so many college graduates do. To keep growing and earning more, we have to be open to new information, be curious, be interested, and ask a lot of questions and then listen to the answers.

10. Be prepared to climb from peak to peak ... our success will never be one long upward progression. Life, as you know, is a series of cycles, ups and downs. When we reach a peak of any type we have to recognize that you have to descend into the valley to get to the next peak. The valley is what makes us stronger.

11. Develop the ability to bounce back ... our ability to bounce back after a temporary defeat or disappointment is what will assure your success in this business. We have to mentally prepare for setbacks and failure and take them in stride.

12. Unlock your in-born creativity ... self made millionaires achieve high levels of success by being innovative, not copying everybody else. Each of us has tremendous amounts of creative potential that we can use to improve every area of our life.

13. Focus on continuous personal development ... all high achievers spend a great deal of time on personal development, losers do not. If you've not committed yourself to being a life-long learner, start today. Whether it be reading books to develop your mindset and skills, listening to CDs, or attending our workshops and retreats ... if you want to earn more you must learn more.

14. Be an unshakable optimist ... self confidence, self esteem, and these other kinds of good thoughts are essential to our success. Very few people are born with them, but they can be developed through practice. Understand that if we look for the best in everybody, and expect to gain something from everything, we'll have the ability to move forward faster.

15. Dedicate yourself to serving others ... if you make great service your obsession, then it's very difficult to ever lose a prospect or client once you've worked with them. Develop the attitude of instead of having a past client you have a client for life.

16. Develop a reputation for speed and dependability ... the easiest, and one of the most valuable, qualities you could develop is a sense of urgency, a drive to more quickly, or simply to get things done now. The smallest percentages of all adults do things quickly and, those

who do, always have the greatest value in a competitive economy.

17. Be 100% honest with yourself and others ... almost all successful businesses ... which leads to a person becoming a millionaire, is built on a high level of trust with everybody you work with. Since life is full of ups and downs, you'll always survive them as long as people trust you because then people can draw on your resources to weather any storm they face.

18. Concentrate on one thing at a time ... set priorities for everything, do the first thing first and do one thing at a time. Focus on the most valuable use of your time to get the highest payoff.

19. Be decisive ... we have to remember that any decision we make is better than no decision at all. Be quick on your feet. You're going to make mistakes, admit to those mistakes and move forward. Be fluid and flexible and open-minded, be decisive.

20. Be disciplined and persistent to win ... do what you should do, when you should do it, whether you like it or not. Then stay at it longer than anybody else and you'll always win.

With all of these said, we have to remember, "Life is not always easy and fair " but since nothing in life is easy and fair let's work beyond what unproductive people do to develop our own self worth and millions.

* * *

I would like to leave you with a list of some final thoughts I have integrated into my life that I believe can help anyone create the life they desire, enjoy and deserve:

- Observe and appreciate each and every moment in life. (Read the book *The Power of Now* by Eckhart Tolle)
- Value your time; use it wisely
- Live a balanced life - Work hard and work smart when you are at work; play or relax when you are not
- Discover who you are and be yourself
- Live with passion
- Be generous but not foolish
- Be grateful for what you have
- Seek opportunities to laugh and smile
- Love easily and without restriction
- Be transparent; allow people to see who you really are
- Be bold and confident
- Find an organizational system and stick with it
- Live with integrity and be impeccable with your word
- Observe the beauty of yourself, your life, your surroundings, and others
- Don't sweat the small stuff
- Try to find peace and happiness in everything you do
- Be nice to everyone
- Look for moments to be of service—and then serve others

With all the love in my heart, I wish every reader of this book a life filled with peace, sobriety, happiness, health, love, and all that you want to create for yourself.

Namaste.

Epilogue

On March 11, 2006, my friend Dieter called to congratulate me for fifteen years of sobriety. During our conversation, he said to me, "My life is better than I ever dreamed it could be." With a smile on my face, I replied with great enthusiasm, "Dieter, did you hear what you just said? Let it resonate. Feel it and know there is more to come. You are going to find yourself, years from now, looking back on your life and saying to yourself, 'How did I get here?' just like the Talking Heads' song. What a beautiful life it is, and there is more to come!"

Years ago, when I was still using, I ran into Dieter at a Grateful Dead show in San Francisco, which, coincidentally, was the same place Dieter had been busted just one year earlier. When I saw him, I was blazing on acid while he was sober and doing the rest of his jail time in a halfway house in Marin County. Unfortunately, I was too high to appreciate randomly running into one of my best friends. In my acid-induced state, I didn't linger with him. I said hello and moved on. I figured I would find him again, somehow, later that night. Busy mingling with thousands of other Dead Heads, completely blazed, I did not run into him again. I did not speak to him for another ten years.

I thought of Dieter out of the blue one day. Wondering how he was doing, I suddenly remembered his parent's phone number. Without delay, I called it from my cell. Unbelievably, the number I dialed was the right number. Although his dad still thought I was the Devil, he gave me Dieter's forwarding number. I immediately called Dieter. I didn't know what to expect, all I knew was I wanted to say, "Hi." That phone conversation turned into so much more.

As we spoke in 2006, Dieter reminisced about that first call. At the time, I was sober, but he was still using. He wanted to get sober, but he thought it was a lost cause. Before hearing my voice that day, he thought it was impossible for anyone as sick as we were to recover. I was the first person he knew that was as bad as he was who managed to stay sober. Finally, for the first time, Dieter had hope that there was a way out for him, too. He confessed, "Rob, when you told me you were sober, I thought, 'If that motherfucker can get sober, then maybe I can, too!'"

I had no idea I'd had such an impact on Dieter's life that day. I thanked him for sharing this story with me. As sober members in The Program, you never know what you may have said or done that has helped someone else in their recovery. **There is a very powerful "ripple effect" in The Program that I believe is the work of God.** He puts us where we need to be at any given time to give or receive His messages. I hope that this book might be a message to readers who need to hear it.

As of 2008, Dieter has almost four years of sobriety and is now, after several previous attempts at sobriety, really putting his life together. It is wonderful to witness the miracle of The Program working in people's lives. Everything happens for a reason. He recently married a woman we attended high school with—Lisa Grantham. I am very grateful to both Dieter and Lisa for their friendship and their willingness to help with this book.

Today, Dieter and I have a great relationship. Other than Adam, most of the other friends I had back in the day are doing their own things, and I have lost touch with them. I have heard stories of their arrests, deaths, and lives of misery. I thank God every day that I have received this gift of sobriety, and I realize that if I do not stay close to God and to The Program, I could easily turn around another 180 degrees in the wrong direction.

Closing Letter from the Author

Dear Reader,

With this book, it is my intention to share *a* way, though not necessarily *the* way, to create sobriety, peace, happiness, security, and wealth. Obviously, my path includes The Program's twelve steps because, for me, it was absolutely the best way to free myself from drugs and/or alcohol abuse and to get my life together. The guidance I received from the book *Alcoholics Anonymous* was, ultimately, what saved my life. Everything that I am and have is a result of that twelve-step program and its suggested reading material.

Additionally, I am forever grateful to The Fellowship of men and women who have loved and supported me; shared their experience, strength, and hope with me, and have helped me become the man I am today. Even today, whenever I go to a 12 Step meeting, I hear something that I can relate to, regardless of what is going on in my life. I often hear something that, by comparison, makes the load I am carrying seem lighter. Hearing other members share their life stories helps me keep my own problems in perspective. At times, I've allowed insignificant problems to take center stage in my life. Listening to others allows me to keep the hangnails of life from taking up too much of my conscious energy. Once I'm aware of how insignificant a grievance is, I can let it go. I have The Fellowship to thank for that.

I do not outline what is already detailed in the book *Alcoholics Anonymous*. You can easily obtain a copy of The Big Book by visiting any Alcoholics Anonymous meeting. To find a meeting, go online to www.aa.org.

The Big Book, as it is called, talks a lot about God. If you have a difficult time with the concept of God, you are not alone. I have witnessed many people struggle with the idea of God. Please do not let this interfere with the book's overall message—that it is possible to live a sober, wonderful life.

In the book, I revealed my flirtation with demonic worship during my teenage years. I shared this incredibly remorseful and shameful past of mine because of the message I hope it sends. **No matter what you have done or how much you may have turned your back on God, He will never turn his back on you. God's love is unconditional!** I know this to be true because of the daily communication I have with God and because of the love I feel in my own spiritual practice. I have come to believe that God's love is a lot like the song, "Amazing Grace." It does not matter if you believe in God or are part of any religion. I am convinced there is a loving God, but I am not a member of any religion and do not believe you need to be to achieve sobriety or happiness. I have seen so many people from all walks of life—both believers and non-believers—achieve the miracle of sobriety, and I believe God favors us all and does not discriminate.

You may find The Big Book a little difficult to read, as I did. It was published in 1939, and the writing style is a bit old fashioned and out of touch. I encourage you to look for the similarities, rather than the differences. That goes for meetings too. Rather than focusing on how your circumstances differ from those at the meeting, focus on what you have in common with them.

Also, if you are a drug addict like me you may be tempted to disregard the advice in The Big Book because it primarily addresses alcohol. Initially, I did not believe that the book's message and program of recovery applied to me. I used drugs more than I drank alcohol. I found all the similarities I needed when I simply replaced the word "alcohol" with "drugs." Once I'd made that substitution, I was able to see more clearly how the book's message of getting and staying sober and about living a sober life of freedom, calmness, and peace could apply to me.

The book, *Alcoholics Anonymous*, offered me an entirely different vision of my life. I was able to eventually envision how to fulfill my every wish in life. The most recognized of The Promises that result from living this new way of life are outlined on pages 83 and 84. They are promised to us once our work on Step 9 is completed.

> *If we are painstaking about this phase of our development, we will be amazed before we are halfway through.*
>
> *We are going to know a new freedom and a new happiness.*
>
> *We will not regret the past nor wish to shut the door on it.*
>
> *We will comprehend the word serenity and we will know peace.*
>
> *No matter how far down the scale we have gone, we will see how our experience can benefit others.*
>
> *That feeling of uselessness and self-pity will disappear.*
>
> *We will lose interest in selfish things and gain interest in our fellows.*
>
> *Self-seeking will slip away.*
>
> *Our whole attitude and outlook on life will change.*
>
> *Fear of people and of economic insecurity will leave us.*

We will intuitively know how to handle situations which used to baffle us.

We will suddenly realize that God is doing for us what we could not do for ourselves.

Are these extravagant promises? We think not. They are being fulfilled among us—sometimes quickly, sometimes slowly. They will always materialize if we work for them.

The first time I read these promises, I was a patient at Coldwater Canyon Hospital. It was like trying to read Japanese. I was unable to connect with any of them. At the time, my only goal was to stop the madness of using drugs. Anything more than that was a pipe dream.

Unfortunately, I notice in The Fellowship of AA that a lot of members either forget these promises, do not believe they will materialize, or simply relish continuing to have problems. They seem to ignore the fact that "The Promises can and will materialize if we work for them."

I once had a conversation with another sober member who had years of sobriety under his belt. His comment was, "I am crazier today than when I was newly sober. The longer I am sober, the crazier I become." To me, statements like that are sad. I believe people hide behind concepts like that to avoid taking responsibility for their lives. These people are missing the biggest gift this program offers us. They do not recognize their **freedom after recovery and the power they have to move on to whatever they wish to create for themselves once they have become sober.**

I also listened to another sober member share with me that he would easily exchange material wealth for spiritual wealth, and I absolutely agreed. However, he went on to share that he believes both are not possible and that you must get rid of one to have the other. This is where *I totally disagreed.* **Why would God not want us to have it all: sobriety, love, peace, health, happiness—and yes, wealth. I believe that God wants us to have it all!**

The Big Book clearly states that by living a life of sobriety and following the suggested steps outlined in the book, we will be given these promises and be able to think and act like normal people. So, if you choose to get sober with the help and support of The Program, The Fellowship, and the book, please, avail yourself of one of the most important messages available—The Promises.

While writing this book, I wanted to be sure to respect the traditions of my twelve-step groups. **Our traditions request that we do not endorse our program in radio, TV, or press. So I want to clarify that this book represents only my experience and is NOT an AA-approved endorsement. I am not an authority on any twelve-step groups, nor do I represent any group as a spokesperson. It is also for this reason that I have omitted my last name, thereby identifying myself with AA anonymously.**

I set up a web site at **www.the180book.com**. At this site, there is a recommended reading list of works by authors dedicated to the paths of recovery, spirituality, self-development, and building wealth.

As stated earlier, the purpose of this book is to offer hope by way of example. If you are struggling with a drug or alcohol addiction and do not see any way out, let me assure you that there *is* a way out. I hope this book and my life are proof. I understand the fear, anger, hopelessness, and frustration you may be feeling. I used to have a serious case of the "fuck-its!" I felt like I was a total loser, a fuck up. I thought, "Fuck it! What is the point?" The point is, if you are fighting a drug or alcohol addiction, you are missing the opportunity to create a life that exceeds your wildest dreams. It is all there waiting for you. Please, go out and get it! I strongly believe that you have no chance if you are loaded! That is the message I hope you get out of this book. You can have a life you always wished for or no life at all, and the choice is yours.

My life is filled with love, security, friends, health, fun, peace, and, yes, an amazing wealthy lifestyle. I want the same for you, and I know that you need only create it for yourself. It is not easy, but I believe it is easier than the alternative. **Working hard to better your life and yourself is easier than constantly working to overcome the problems you create for yourself with drugs.** It's easier than dealing with a nightmare life of chaos and misery. It's easier than living with shame and guilt over the pain you bring on yourself and those who love you. And it's far more rewarding and pleasurable than chasing a drug-induced high. If you've "crossed the line" in your addiction, then you can no longer attain the high you are seeking anyway. If you get sober, you can have something even better. You can create a beautiful life! I hope you believe me. Most importantly, I hope you believe in yourself! Visualize it! Feel it. Internalize the feeling of success! Trust me. It's better than any artificial high. Get pumped for life and for massive success! It's waiting for you. Just go and get it!

Buy this book on-line:

www.the180book.com

Visit our Sober Living Home in Malibu, Ca.

www.theserrahouse.com
310-850-3260

Read or write a testimonial on the Facebook fan page:

www.Facebook.com/180Degrees

Glossary of Drug Jargon

Bags– Bags used for holding drugs.

Basing – Free-basing or smoking crack, meth, cocaine or heroin.

Bindles – Paper folded envelopes used to hold drugs in powder form.

Binged – Taking a lot of drugs over a long period.

Blaze – Being high on acid.

Basing – Cooked cocaine that is used for smoking.

Blow – Cocaine.

Bolted – To flee quickly.

Bowl – A bowl in a pipe.

Brown – Heroin.

Bust/busted – Caught with or doing drugs.

Cook rock/melting rock – The act of heating cocaine into freebase or crack form.

Crack master – Nickname for someone who does a lot of crack.

Crack – Form of cooked freebase for smoking cocaine.

Crack house – A place where you can sell and buy crack.

Crank – Meth.

Crash – Coming off of drugs.

Dope fiend – Person addicted to dope.

Dosed – Taking acid.

Drop acid/tabs – Drop pieces of LSD into one's mouth.

Fifty-piece – $50 worth of crack or cocaine.

Hit of acid – Dose of LSD.
Hit/take a hit – Taking drugs.
Holding – A person who has drugs on them.
Hitting it hard – Using drugs frequently and excessively.
Jones – Anxiety about getting more drugs and needing them badly.
Narc – To tell on a drug user, or an undercover Narcotics Agent.
Narced/narcing – Snitching on someone else.
Newcomer – Someone new in The Program.
Partying/partied – Getting high, doing drugs.
Pop – Take pills.
Rig – Needle and syringe.
Rock – Cooked cocaine, like freebase or crack.
Scamming – Do a deal to take advantage of someone.
Scored/copped – Make a deal and get drugs.
Shrooms/magic mushrooms – Hallucinogenic mushrooms.
Slamming/ shooting/shooting up/sticking/stick – Injecting drugs.
Slip – To lose continuous sobriety by getting high/drinking.
Sparked up – Light a cigarette or pipe.
Speedball – A mix of coke and heroin.
Sponsors – People who guide new members thru the 12 Step Program.
Spun – Going crazy/wild.
Staying clean – To be off of drugs.
Stoned – High on drugs.
The Fellowship – Members who participate in a 12 step group.
The Program – The 12 steps and AA's goals.
Toasted – Completely stoned and out of it.
Trip/tripping – Taking acid.
Weed/pot/buds/joint/herb – Marijuana.
Whacked – Kill someone.
Whacked out – Very high on drugs/not in control.

APPENDIX I
Recovery and Rehabilitation Centers

The following is a list of questions to consider when selecting a substance abuse treatment center:

- Does the rehab center accept your insurance? If not, will they work with you on a payment plan or find other means of support for you?

- Is the center run by state-accredited licensed and/or trained professionals?

- Is the facility clean, organized, and well-run?

- Does the substance abuse rehab program encompass the full range of needs of the individual (medical - including addressing the issues of those with infectious diseases, psychological - including addressing issues of mental illness, social, vocational, legal, etc.)?

- Does the drug rehab program also address sexual orientation and physical disabilities as well as provide age, gender, and culturally appropriate treatment services?

- Are long-term aftercare support and/or guidance encouraged, provided, and maintained after the recovering individual leaves the rehab program?

- Is there ongoing assessment of an individual's treatment plan to ensure it meets changing needs?

- Does the substance abuse program employ strategies to engage and keep individuals in longer-term treatment, if necessary, to increase the likelihood of success?

- Does the program offer counseling (individual or group) and other behavioral therapies to enhance the individual's ability to function in the family/community?

- Does the program offer medication as part of its treatment regimen, if appropriate?

- Is there ongoing monitoring of possible relapse to help guide patients back to abstinence?

- Does the center offer family members any services or referrals to assist them in understanding addiction and the recovery process so that they can better support the recovering individual?

Treatment Facility Resources

The Betty Ford Center
(800) 434-7365
www.bettyfordcenter.org/

ChangePoint
(503) 253-5954
www.changepointinc.com/

Clare Foundation, Inc.
(866) 452-5273
www.clarefoundation.org

Hazelden
(800) 257-7810
www.hazelden.org

Matrix Institute
(800) 310-7700
www.matrixinstitute.org

New Beginnings
www.nbrecovery.net

Promises
(866) 390-2340
www.promises.com

The Salvation Army
Adult Rehabilitation Centers (ARC)
Harbor Lights Centers
Search for an ARC or Harbor Lights Center in your area:
www.satruck.org/FindARC.aspx

SAMHSA (Substance Abuse & Mental Health Services Administration U.S. Department of Health and Human Services)
SUBSTANCE ABUSE TREATMENT FACILITY LOCATOR
www.findtreatment.samhsa.gov

US Drug Rehab Centers
(866) 449-1490 www.usdrugrehabcenters.com

Recovery Support and Information

AddictionSearch.com
Nationwide Addiction Assistance Helpline
(800) 559-9503
www.addictionsearch.com

Alcoholics Anonymous
(212) 647-1680
www.aa.org

Cocaine Anonymous
(800) 347-8998
www.ca.org

Crystal Meth Anonymous
(213) 488-4455
www.crystalmeth.org

Narcotics Anonymous
(818) 773-9999
www.na.org

National Council on Alcoholism and Drug Dependence
www.ncadd.org

National Institute on Drug Abuse
(800) 662-4357
www.nida.nih.gov
teens.drugabuse.gov

U.S. Department of Health and Human Services / SAMHSA's National Clearinghouse for Alcohol & Drug Information / RADAR Network (Regional Alcohol and Drug Abuse Resources)
(800) 729-6686
ncadi.samhsa.gov

Support to Stop Smoking

Nicotine Anonymous
www.nicotine-anonymous.org

American Cancer Society
(800) 227-2345
www.cancer.org

National Cancer Institute
(800) 422-6237
www.cancer.gov

Support for Friends and Family

Al-Anon/Alateen
(888) 4AL-ANON
www.al-anon.alateen.org

Families Anonymous
(800) 736-9805
www.familiesanonymous.org

About the Author

After seven years of considerable struggle, at the age of twenty-two (March 11, 1991), Robert made the choice to be sober from drugs and alcohol, enabling him to turn his life around *180 Degrees*. As a result of his commitment to his recovery and self-improvement, Robert became a millionaire by the age of thirty.

Eternally grateful to everyone who helped him become and remain sober, Robert felt compelled to reach out to other addicts and wrote *180 Degrees* in hopes that his story would inspire others battling addiction to find their own success. Robert continues to be of service as a philanthropist and active community member. He has shared his fascinating story on panels, in high schools, juvenile detention centers and throughout his community. He continues to be an active participant in the twelve-step community.

Robert has over eighteen years of experience in real estate, is considered one of the nation's leading agents, and has been featured in print and on television.

Robert resides happily and soberly in Los Angeles, California with his wife, Halle, and sons, Skyler and Grayson.

You can email Rob at: rob@the180book.com

Rob's Recommended Reading List

Author: Alcoholics Anonymous
Title: The Big Book

Author: Rhonda Byrne
Title: The Secret

Author: T. Harv Eker
Title: Secrets of the Millionaire Mind

Author: Neale Donald Walsch
Title: Friendship With God: An Uncommon Dialogue
Title: Conversations With God: An Uncommon Dialogue, Book 3
Title: Conversations With God: An Uncommon Dialogue, Book 2
Title: Conversations With God: An Uncommon Dialogue, Book 1

Author: Dr. Wayne W. Dyer
Title: The Power of Intention
Title: There's a Spiritual Solution to Every Problem
Title: You'll See It When You Believe It
Title: Wisdom of the Ages

Title: Your Sacred Self

Title: Your Erroneous Zones

Title: Real Magic: Creating Miracles in Everyday Life

Author: Anthony Robbins

Title: Unleash the Power Within:
Personal Coaching to Transform Your Life!

Title: Unlimited Power:
The New Science of Personal Achievement

Title: Awaken the Giant Within:
How to Take Immediate Control of Your Mental,
Emotional, Physical, & Financial Destiny

Author: Eckhart Tolle

Title: Practicing the Power of Now: Essential Teachings,
Meditations, and Exercises from the Power of Now

Title: The Power of Now: A Guide to Spiritual Enlightenment

Author: Lama Surya Das

Title: Awakening the Buddhist Heart

Title: Awakening to the Sacred

Title: Awakening the Buddha Within

Author: Dr. Stephen R Covey

Title: First Things First

Title: Principle-Centered Leadership

Title: The 7 Habits for Highly Effective People

Author: Deepak Chopra

Title: Creating Affluence

Title: Seven Spiritual Laws of Success

Title: Ageless Body, Timeless Mind

Author: Dalai Lama

Title: How to Practice: The Way to a Meaningful Life

Title: The Art of Happiness

Title: The Meaning of Life

Author: Brian Tracy

Title: Time Power: A Proven System for Getting More Done in Less Time

Title: Create Your Own Future: How to Master the 12 Critical Factors of Unlimited Success

---

Author: Phillip C. McGraw, Ph.D.

Title: Relationship Rescue: A Seven-Step Strategy for Reconnecting with Your Partner

Title: Life Strategies: Doing What Works, Doing What Matters

Author: Richard Carlson, Ph.D.

Title: Don't Sweat the Small Stuff at Work

Title: Don't Sweat the Small Stuff About Money

Title: Don't Sweat the Small Stuff in Love

Title: Don't Worry, Make Money

Title: Don't Sweat the Small Stuff - and it's all small stuff

---

Author: Napoleon Hill

Title: Think & Grow Rich

Author: Robert T Kiyosaki
Title: Retire Young Retire Rich
Title: Cashflow Quadrant
Title: Rich Dad's Guide to Investing
Title: Rich Dad Poor Dad

Author: M. Scott Peck, M.D.
Title: The Road Less Traveled

Author: Norman Vincent Peale
Title: The Power of Positive Thinking

Author: Earl Nightingale
Title: Lead the Field

Author: Dr. Maoshing Ni
Title: Secrets of Longevity: Hundreds of Ways to Live to Be 100

Author: David Joseph Schwartz
Title: The Magic of Thinking Big

Author: Richard Templar
Title: The Rules of Money:
How to Make it and How to Hold on to It

Author: Jim Stovall
Title: The Ultimate Gift

Author: Don Miguel Ruiz
Title: The Four Agreements:
A Practical Guide to Personal Freedom

Author: John Gray, Ph.D.
Title: Men are from Mars, Women are from Venus

Author: Michael E. Gerber
Title: The E Myth Revisited: Why Most Small Businesses Don't Work and What to Do about it

---

Author: Gary Keller
Title: The Millionaire Real Estate Investor

Author: George S. Clason
Title: The Richest Man in Babylon

Author: Gerald Coffee
Title: Beyond Survival

Author: Emmet Fox
Title: The Sermon on the Mount

Author: Viktor E. Frankl
Title: Man's Search for Meaning

Author: Jack L. Canfield
Title: Mark Victor Hansen and Les Hewitt, The Power of Focus

Author: Jack L. Canfield and Mark Victor Hansen
Title: Chicken Soup for the Soul

Author: Ken Blanchard and Sheldon Bowles
Title: Gung Ho!

Author: Robert G. Allen
Title: Creating Wealth

Author: Mary Buffet and David Clark
Title: The New Buffettology: The Profen Techniques for Investing Successfully in Changing Markets that have made Warren Buffet the World's Most Famous Investor

---

Author: Robert G. Hagstrom
Title: The Warren Buffett Way

Author: Peter Lynch
Title: Beating the Street

Author: Dolf De Roos, Ph.D.
Title: Real Estate Riches

Author: Charles Schwab
Title: Charles Schwab's New Guide to Financial Independence: Practical Solutions for Busy People

---

Author: Morgan Westerman
Title: The Interview with God

Author: Mike Ferry
Title: Real Estate According to Mike Ferry

180 Degrees

Online Orders

Please go to: www.The180Book.com.

There is a secure PayPal checkout for your purchase.

Postal Orders

Mail checks to: PO BOX 174, Pacific Palisades, CA 90272. Please fill out your information below.

Name: _____

Address: _____

City: _____ State: _____ Zip: _____

Telephone: _____

Email Address: _____

Sales Tax

Please add 9.25% for all orders shipped to a California address.

Shipping

U.S. orders: $4.00 for the first book and $2.00 for each additional.

International orders: $9.00 for the first book and $5.00 for each additional.

Please call, 310-850-3260, with any questions. Thank you!

180 Degrees

Online Orders

Please go to: www.The180Book.com.

There is a secure PayPal checkout for your purchase.

Postal Orders

Mail checks to: PO BOX 174, Pacific Palisades, CA 90272. Please fill out your information below.

Name: _____

Address: _____

City: _____ State:_____ Zip: _____

Telephone:_____

Email Address: _____

Sales Tax

Please add 9.25% for all orders shipped to a California address.

Shipping

U.S. orders: $4.00 for the first book and $2.00 for each additional.

International orders: $9.00 for the first book and $5.00 for each additional.

Please call, 310-850-3260, with any questions. Thank you!

180 Degrees

Online Orders

Please go to: www.The180Book.com.

There is a secure PayPal checkout for your purchase.

Postal Orders

Mail checks to: PO BOX 174, Pacific Palisades, CA 90272. Please fill out your information below.

Name: _____

Address: _____

City: _____ State:_____ Zip: _____

Telephone:_____

Email Address: _____

Sales Tax

Please add 9.25% for all orders shipped to a California address.

Shipping

U.S. orders: $4.00 for the first book and $2.00 for each additional.

International orders: $9.00 for the first book and $5.00 for each additional.

Please call, 310-850-3260, with any questions. Thank you!